M000014783

Faithful Sexuality

Faithful Sexuality

Human Stories about Holy Sexuality as the Beloved People of God

By
GARY L. GRAFWALLNER

WIPF & STOCK · Eugene, Oregon

FAITHFUL SEXUALITY
Human Stories about Holy Sexuality as the Beloved People of God

Copyright © 2019 Gary L. Grafwallner. All rights reserved. Except for brief
quotations in critical publications or reviews, no part of this book may
be reproduced in any manner without prior written permission from the
publisher. Write: Permissions, Wipf and Stock Publishers, 199 W. 8th Ave.,
Suite 3, Eugene, OR 97401.

Wipf & Stock
An Imprint of Wipf and Stock Publishers
199 W. 8th Ave., Suite 3
Eugene, OR 97401

www.wipfandstock.com

PAPERBACK ISBN: 978-1-5326-9782-1
HARDCOVER ISBN: 978-1-5326-9783-8
EBOOK ISBN: 978-1-5326-9784-5

Manufactured in the U.S.A.   11/01/19

Dedicated with my heartfelt gratitude to Gail L. Grafwallner,
wife, companion, best friend

"I ask you my sisters and brothers to give God your bodies, as an act of intelligent worship do not be conformed to the world but transformed by the renewal of your minds that you may prove in practice the will of God is good and acceptable and perfect."

—ROMANS 12:1–2

"Do you love me more than these?"
"You know . . . I love you."
"Do you love me?"
"Certainly you know everything. You know I love you."
"Do you love me? . . ."

—JOHN 21:15–17

Contents

Introduction

WHEN I TOLD A friend and colleague I was writing on sexuality and the Christian faith he said, "Gary, I think the church should have a moratorium on all speaking and writing about sex for at least one hundred years given all the damage it's done. Furthermore, the world probably is not interested." That was a sobering rejoinder to what follows. He's right, "the world" probably isn't interested. John the Evangelist defines "the world" as all those individuals, groups, systems, that are against "the God who became a human being and lived among us."

On my long Ignatian retreat, one of the presenters said, "The kingdom or queendom or reign of God is about right relationships with God, others, and ourselves." I am writing from the perspective of my own life and faith as a Christian man, husband, father, grandfather, pastor, priest, and theologian. This book also reflects my own journey of learning, coping, and understanding as a married person.

I have seen the sexual revolution, the advent of the pill, and the Implant RU234. Some Christian youth in the parishes I served are sexually active in high school, but the vast majority are sexually active in college. A friend just told me at a media conference he attended, 90 percent of the actors in relationships in sitcoms and movies go to bed on the first or second date. Abortion has become a means of birth control for thousands in the state of Oregon. More and more couples who come for premarital counseling are living together. They're not only in their twenties but in their seventies, trying to avoid tax penalties from bad laws. Fifty-one percent of all the marriages in Oregon will end in divorce. Sperm banks, surrogate partner/parents, and in-vitro fertilization are becoming more accepted means of becoming a parent. Domestic partners want their relationships blessed. Unsafe sex feeds the spread of various STDs and HIV. Sex continues to sell music, cars, clothes, food, cologne, sports, liquor, travel—you name it. Transgender people are also more public about their changes.

Except for the Christian right and fundamentalists, the church has for the most part been silent during the revolution. Rules and guilt no longer seem to control parishioners' behavior. In society, people seem to choose their own course. My sense is that there is more public variety manifest around sexual behavior. The Episcopalians, Lutherans, Methodists, Presbyterians and Baptists have taken heat for their churches' social statements on sexuality. They're too liberal for some and too traditional for others. I wonder if as people of faith we simply endorse the world's agenda.

I have listened to singles, marrieds, gays, lesbians, teens, senior citizens, and parents who were people of faith but who struggled with their feelings, relationships, and their behavior around sexual matters. What is acceptable to Jesus? What honors or pleases God? So I decided to share the stories, experiences, and wisdom of hundreds of people who have taught me. This is not a pious dogmatic treatise, but my own pastoral reflections on the implications of God's call in matters of faith and sex. It's a chance to think out loud with you and I hope, in the process, provide a catalyst for conversation and some teaching on what it means to live in God's light and reflect God's love in a holy and hopeful community.

Everything that follows is true, although details have been changed to preserve confidentiality. If you recognize yourself or someone you know in these pages, thank you for sharing your struggles and wisdom with me. I am forever grateful that God made us sexual beings and that we are each unique, awesome, and good.

GLG

Just How Sexual Are You?

I REMEMBER BEING AT a four-day workshop on money sponsored by a local Presbyterian congregation. My small group included Mary, a therapist and wife of a timber industry magnate. She was a vivacious but unpretentious woman in her early sixties who was beautiful both inside and out. She said, "One morning as I showered, I stood next to my husband who was in his seventies. He was tall, lean, and well-muscled. He swam, played tennis, and was an avid walker. I was struck by the beauty of his body given his years. Later at breakfast we were sitting together and I said, 'David you are quite sexy.'" I thought to myself, "He is, but so are you."

How comfortable are you with your body? I've noticed that people who are overweight often wear their shirts out. They prefer large sweaters or loose-fitting clothes. People who are extremely thin may wear tights or layered clothing, turtleneck shirts, and long-sleeve sweaters with jeans. Those who are growing bald may comb their hair forward or purchase a hairpiece or get a hair transplant. People who can afford it may get plastic surgery for a facelift, a tummy tuck, to have their wrinkles removed, or to their change breast size.

Someone suggested to me that a helpful exercise is to spend fifteen minutes in front of the mirror periodically looking at your body front view, side view, and back profile. Ask yourself, which parts do you like? Why? Which parts do you dislike? I remember an elderly Hispanic woman who looked at the stretch marks on her legs and great belly. She said, "I've earned every one of these bearing nine children." Her comment gave me a lot to think about. Are you able to give thanks for your body?

I spent a four-day weekend for continuing education at the Vancouver School of Theology with Walter Wink and June Kerner Wink. He is a New Testament theologian and teacher of Koine Greek. She teaches movement. Before we would do Scripture study with Walter, June would open us up to the Word by getting us in touch with our bodies so we would come to Scripture study using both hemispheres of our brains.

June told us how she felt terrible about her body as a teenager. She said, "I had a big nose, a flat chest, wide hips, and feet like shovels. I was taller than any of the boys in my grade." Her sister's teasing did not help, and she hated her body for years. After going through a painful divorce, she married Walter, who taught at Union Seminary in New York. Being raised a Methodist preacher's daughter, she had "gone forth to the altar, confessed her sins, professed her faith," but she said, "I never felt God's grace." She was spiritually drying up in this academic community that was "all head, little heart, and no spirit" when she signed up for a class on movement at a local community college. This was not a dance class but one where you freely interpreted the music you heard. She said, "It was the first time I experienced grace. I bent, moved, stretched, twirled, sank, and arose. I felt free and positive about my body, open and playful as I moved to the music." She went back to take a second class, and a third and then a fourth. Finally, she went to a master teacher in New York City. Now she travels with her husband doing workshops and teaches others how to relax, to let go, and personally interpret the music or words they are hearing.

Something June invited us to do while we were with her was to bless our bodies. She told us how we neglect our bodies and take them for granted instead of blessing them. Each of us lay on our backs with enough space between each person so that no one touched the other. Then we closed out eyes and silently moved our hands over each part of our bodies, pausing to ponder how wonderfully we are created and then to give a blessing and say, "Thanks." It was powerful to move from our toes, to feet, to ankles, to calves, to thighs, and then think about how each part functioned and was God-given. We blessed our genitals and pelvises, hips and waists and stomachs. We thought about the organs we take for granted like the skin, heart, lungs, liver, and kidneys, pancreas and colon. We touched our lower and upper backs, our breasts and chests, collar bones, shoulders, biceps, triceps, forearms, wrists, hands, thumbs, and fingers. Finally, we came to our necks and heads. We touched our lips and mouths and teeth, our eyes and ears, and noses, our foreheads and the crowns of our heads. We each had thought about our total selves and blessed them. It was an amazing experience to name and picture each part and say, "This is of God. Behold, this is good. This is to be cherished."

One of my colleagues was giving a lecture when he said, "Our sexuality includes all that we are, not just our 'gender and genitals.'" In other words, our sexuality includes not only our anatomy and physique, but also our scent. The way we sit, walk, and cross our legs. The colors and clothes we choose and how they fit, our hairstyles and cuts, whether we shave our heads or pluck our eyebrows or grow a beard are all part of our sexuality. The jewelry we wear, a tattoo, even our laugh is part of our sexuality.

According to the New Testament, all who are baptized into Christ are members of the body of Christ and a temple of the Holy Spirit. We are joined to God through Jesus Christ. We live in God, and God lives in us. Food and drink, work and rest, prayer and play all contribute to our appearance, attitude, and sense of well-being. The way we treat our bodies colors how we feel about ourselves and our sexuality. Years ago, someone gave me a tiny wood plaque that reads, "If I would have known I was going to live this long, I would have taken better care of myself." "God created us male and female." "We are sexual beings and we are good."

QUESTIONS FOR REFLECTION

- Do you celebrate the goodness of your sexuality?

- What might it mean to you personally when in the New Testament we are told, "Your bodies are not your own to do with as you please for you were redeemed for a price. Therefore glorify God with your bodies"?

PRAYER

- Creator God, thank you for the goodness of flesh and creating us sexual beings. Help us to respect and cherish our bodies which are your creation. Amen.

Touching Appropriately

NEVA WAS A WIDOW in the first parish I served. In her seventies, she lived on a railroader's tiny pension plus Social Security in a small house on a hill outside the city limits. She heated her house with wood, had no indoor plumbing, and got water from a catch fed by a spring that ran eleven months of the year. She gardened, grew flowers, and made all sorts of craft art out of stuff others discarded.

Neva had one daughter who lived in the middle of the state, but there wasn't a lot of contact. I was unofficially adopted as her son. She would drop by the office to bring me flowers, baked goods, or to gift me with a piece of pottery or small craft item she had fashioned. It quickly became apparent that she was lonely.

One evening during a week my wife was out of town, Neva treated me to a homemade chicken dinner with all the trimmings. It was obvious she had pulled out all the stops. I felt as though I had been treated like royalty. As I got up to leave, I gave her a hug. A tear came to her eyes so I asked, "Neva, what's wrong?" "You are the first man who's hugged me since my husband died." I asked her how long ago that had been and she told me slightly more than twenty years had passed since his death. Can you imagine not receiving a hug for twenty years? I wonder how any people who knew her even suspected her loneliness.

Ten years later I attended a Leadership Skills Institute sponsored by the Episcopal Church. A lot of it dealt with small group process. After one week together, the normal social barriers were down and all the participants were quite open about expressing their feelings. One facilitator warned us about what she referred to as the "TLF" syndrome. She went on to explain the way some people functioned behaviorally was as follows: "I touch you. I love you. I f—k you." Not only in that group but in any relationship, we need to be aware of all the messages our touch can communicate or miscommunicate.

I had a very talented creative colleague who couldn't keep his hands off female parishioners. This was many years before the Clarence Thomas/Anita Hill hearings. He denied this was a problem even after women began to call the bishop's office. He and his wife were asked to seek out a counselor. It was rumored he and his wife were having problems in their marriage. He continued to make light of his inappropriate remarks and behavior. When other women complained that his behavior continued, ultimately he had to resign since he couldn't abide by the church's guidelines. He became a fireman. A pastor had become a predator.

All clergy and religious church workers have been required by our bishop to attend a sexual harassment workshop because of all the litigation which the church is involved with. This was a professional consciousness-raiser and a corporate measure to protect the church's backside. Many of my colleagues will no longer pick up children or hug or kiss children, teens, or adults out of fear of a lawsuit.

Some would say the pendulum has swung too far in the other direction. But last year a female colleague who is a single woman serving a parish as the sole pastor wrote an excellent newsletter article, "Touch in the Congregation." She indicated many men seem to think they can hug or touch her every time they see her. Her viewpoint is, "It's not always welcome or appropriate." She was asking for a new sensitivity and respect on the part of all congregational members. "I don't want to violate your space but I also need appropriate boundaries to protect myself," she wrote to her congregation.

Can there be a happy medium? Perhaps we need to ask permission to discover whether someone is open to a hug or kiss. That may seem unnatural if you're a hugger, but it's also a safeguard. We dare not assume everyone needs or welcomes our touch when we want to demonstrate our affection. I believe it's better to check it out than be burned. But in the spontaneity of the moment sometimes I still forget, catch myself, and apologize.

QUESTIONS FOR REFLECTION

- When you feel you want to touch a particular person, ask yourself what you think your motivation is. Is the feeling mutual? Are there potential dangers?

- What kind of touch do you welcome? When? From whom?

- If you are uncomfortable with someone's touch, are you able to say so clearly?

PRAYER

- Loving God, help us not to misuse the gift of touch. Let all touch be a sign of human and holy affection and your care. Amen.

Celibacy Is Not the Same as Being Single

IN SOME PARTS OF the church, celibacy still is lifted up as a calling. Celibacy is choosing for the sake of Jesus and the reign of God to neither marry nor have sexual relations. According to the teaching of Jesus and the New Testament, celibacy is a gift. I believe it should not be legislated by a church hierarchy. Within Roman Catholicism over ten thousand priests have left the priesthood because they met someone, fell in love, and decided to marry. Within my tradition, the calling to be a pastor and the calling to marriage are not mutually exclusive. I believe celibacy can be personally claimed by some people as part of our response to the Risen One's invitation to become a follower. To be celibate is to choose Jesus as "one's partner" and to offer one's whole life in service of God within the church and for the world.

I asked Tim how he dealt with his sexuality as a single celibate priest. He had asked me whether being married was a help or a hindrance to my ministry. I told him for me it has been a great help. He was impressed by the comments I made about my wife. He, in turn, shared how he had fallen in love twice but had chosen not to marry or renounce his priestly vows. He said, "I feel like the hereafter is more important in my choice than the present." I asked him to explain and he replied, "Marriage is for this life and the here and now. I have chosen for eternity. In heaven there will be no such thing as marriage. Sometimes the grass looks greener if you are married. I still get periodic cases of feeling horny but they pass."

As we were driving in his car, Tim noticed a couple of very attractive women. He said, "Beautiful hair and curves. I like to think of it as an appreciation of the aesthetic." I chuckled and he said, "What do you think, Gary?" I replied, "For me that would be a rationalization." He smiled and said, "It does help me to get by. Looking doesn't have to be lusting." We both laughed.

Bob, Kate, and Susan have embraced the gift of celibacy. Bob is a Roman Catholic priest who serves a congregation. Kate, a nun, serves the larger church in spirituality. Susan, a nun, works in peace and justice ministries. Bob, while never marrying, knows a great deal about family systems, marriage, and teens. He is an excellent counselor. He enjoys cooking, skiing, and a good party. Kate listens to God and helps people discern God's leading. She is one of the most holy, human, transparent, joy-filled people I know. She enjoys music and theater. Susan has worked with refugees, migrants, and native peoples while also being active in education and advocacy work for Christian nonviolence. She enjoys travel, dance, and ethnic music. Kate and Bob have said they would enjoy being parents and grandparents.

God is the first love of Bob, Kate, and Susan. Their lives, energy, and ministry flow from their relationship with God. Make no mistake. They struggle with pride and loneliness. They get their feelings hurt. They wrestle with how to redirect their sexual drives. Sometimes it is particularly difficult to not be able to give their bodies and themselves to another person. They frequently work too hard and their lives get out of balance. At times they struggle with self-doubt. Nevertheless, you cannot be with them for a short period of time before you sense their deep walk with God. They have made me realize that celibacy is both a gift and a choice. It is sort of like fasting from having genital relations for the sake of their ministries, knowing they do this with others and are not alone. The Holy One is their food and drink. They live with a sense of detachment and are free to give, serve, and even relocate in ways that those of us who are married or who parent children are often unable or unwilling to do.

QUESTIONS FOR REFLECTION

- Have you ever considered that some people's singleness or your own may not be a burden to discard but an asset to be embraced and a gift to be capitalized upon?

PRAYER

- Spirit of God, thank you for those whose grace gift is celibacy and the freedom which permits them to serve God in some special ways. Amen.

Lips Are Made for the Sport of It

I WAS PICKING UP my wife from a bridal shower and arrived early. Not all the presents had been opened, so I got to see some of the serious ones as well as the light-hearted ones. The bride-to-be opened one that contained a jar of flavored body lotion. On the first night of her honeymoon or some other night when she was feeling especially amorous, evidently she was to rub her body with this stuff and then in the heat of passion her partner was supposed to lick it off. To me it sounded like it would make the bed sticky, but then who knows? Everyone laughed and she blushed as the gift's use was explained.

Do you remember your first kiss as a teen? Some of you may have practiced on a friend, or sibling, or doll before the real event. Or you may have stood in front of a bedroom mirror and puckered up your lips, half open, held your breath, and slowly exhaled through your nostrils. My first kiss was with a girl following a school dance. It was awkward and I felt self-conscious. I think I recall feigning excitement, but I was unsure of myself and my feelings for the girl I kissed. Early in my life there had been all kinds of kisses: kisses of welcome, kisses of comfort after a bad fall from a trike, kisses of endearment, bedtime kisses from my mother, and a variety of kisses from my maternal grandmother, favorite aunts, and one or two older cousins. A romantic kiss is quite different.

To return to the flavored body lotion—can you imagine what it would be like to have your entire body kissed if you were freshly bathed? How does the thought of your beloved kissing you starting with your toes and moving up your body until they finally reach your neck, ears, lips, and forehead make you feel? Could you lie back and receive that gift as their lips lovingly honored each part of your body? It would certainly make me feel very affirmed. Come to think of it, we do this with babies, but I wonder how many of us experience this as adults?

Within the early church "the kiss of peace" was practiced between believers during worship. One New Testament letter says, "Greet one another with the kiss of peace." It apparently was a sign of reconciliation and unity in Christ as well as of friendship. In different congregations I suspect people get into this practice in varying degrees based on the nature of congregational life and also the history of the relationship. Nowadays we call it the "Sharing of the Peace." It involves the verbal greeting, "The Peace of the Lord be with you," between pastor and congregation and then between the members. It is often followed by a handshake, hug, or kiss. "The Peace" often is shared between spouses, parents, and children, friends, singles, and marrieds. At congregations where I served, some Sundays people get carried away and newcomers are either put off or drawn in by it. One of the observations the Greco-Roman world made of the early Christians was, "See how they love one another."

It's amazing what we can communicate through a kiss: welcome, playfulness, comfort, reassurance, affection, tenderness, curious exploration, a sensuous invitation, deep passion, fatigue, a farewell. A coworker of mine once said, "Lips are made for the sport of it." Ah, how true and so much more.

QUESTIONS FOR REFLECTION

- Whose kisses do you yearn for? Have you told them?
- Who might yearn for your kisses? Have you asked them?

PRAYER

- Extravagant God, thank you for creating us with lips. No matter what our age or gender, we all need to give and receive kisses. It's a great way to communicate. Amen.

Unevenly Yoked
or Married to a Non-Christian

SARAH WAS BAPTIZED AS a child but never really nurtured in the church. Her father was an agnostic and her mother was a practical atheist. Consequently, she was pretty much left to spiritually fend for herself. As a child she attended Sunday church school occasionally with her friends. As a teenager, she would attend a church youth group if one of her friends did. Her college years included the typical rebellions. She experimented with alternative lifestyles and ended up living with a group of people. Eventually she married Sam. At that time religion was not important.

Sam was raised within the Orthodox Church. He was an altar boy but he got turned off as a young teen and left the church. He has never really gone back. He's not antireligious, just indifferent. His attitude is basically, "If you need it, fine, but I don't and I won't." He jokes about being the black sheep of his family. He had been a good provider, and a faithful husband.

As a young adult Sarah's involvement in the church was sporadic. Sarah pretty much went along with her early childhood pattern regarding religion and the church until she had a powerful religious dream in which Jesus spoke to her. That dream became a turning point which marked a conversion in her life. She began to discuss spiritual ideas with friends whom she respected. She started praying and reading devotional books, the Bible, and theology. She had lots of questions and became hungry to know God. She started participating in an evangelical conservative Bible study.

Slowly she began to visit various congregations to find something for her children and herself. She has continued to blossom and grow, and, at times, thrive. Currently she is active in a congregation as a follower of Jesus.

Her husband, however, has not followed her lead. He is the same conscientious, hardworking, fun loving, thrifty guy. He is a good man, but not perfect. Her Christian faith and growth have at times caused tensions around parenting, finances, extended family, and goals for the future. One day we were visiting and she freely admitted, "Knowing what I know now, if I had to do it over again, I would probably not marry Sam. When we met and began a relationship, I was not a practicing Christian." Lots of other women and some men might say something similar. It can be hard pulling together when you're "unevenly yoked."

One of the temptations in being married to a non-Christian, according to Sarah, is to avoid making waves. "You try not to bring up the subject of God or the church or the Bible or prayer or giving money."

I've watched many people tiptoe around spiritual things with a non-believing spouse. The danger I see in being quiet about your beliefs is you may end up compromising your own relationship with God but also your spouse or any children. If we lie to keep the peace at home, then everybody loses. God wants to be our first love, not just an equal to our spouse, children, partner, or parents.

I know a single woman who has made a commitment to her boyfriend. He is capable, intelligent, and likable. He is very clear about not sharing her belief in God. Now, it doesn't mean he won't change, but she cannot assume that. The belief that God was in Jesus is basic to who she is. I can see potential problems down the road if they decide to marry or have children. Jesus was very clear that loyalty to him and the Father takes precedence over loyalty to our family. One of the wrinkles in this scenario is that the woman, like Sarah, is not clear in her own mind about how important she wants God to be in her life.

I grew up in a household where my own father was not a practicing Christian, yet my mother was an active church member.

Early on I became aware of my mother's frustration and the pain and disappointment a spiritually divided household can cause. Although my mother taught us to be Christians, my father's lack of involvement undermined her example.

One summer I was hiking in Scotland with a man close to sixty. Ken said, "My wife is not a Christian, but I hope she will become one someday. My daughters are not Christians either, although they're both spiritual. They're young and need a little hardship in their lives before they'll feel a need to turn to God. My wife, on the other hand, has always been a loner. She suffers from low self-esteem. I have asked a few trusted friends to pray for her, but not publicly." Can you hear the ache, the yearning, the hope that perhaps one day we who share human love will share divine love before one of us dies? When a couple shares not only their lives but God's life, it can open up sharing more deeply in many areas.

QUESTIONS FOR REFLECTION

- If you are married to "a good person" who is not Christian, how has their lack of faith or a different belief from your own beliefs impacted the marriage?

- Is there someone who might pray for them or engage them in conversation and invite them to consider the words and life of Jesus?

PRAYER

- Maker of all, help me to not get in the way of your efforts to reach my beloved nonbeliever but to be a loving and truthful channel of your grace, along with others, to them. Amen.

Single, Sexual, and Whole

A PROFESSIONAL WOMAN WHO lives in another state usually stops for an overnight stay at our house on her way to visit her parents in British Columbia. She is in her forties, a practicing Christian who has never married. She has been very involved in her local congregation and its ministry in the community. This year during her visit I inquired if I could ask her a personal question based on our long years of friendship. "Sure," she replied.

"How do you deal with your sexual needs as a single Christian woman?"

She blushed and I assured her she could pass on the question. Then she braced herself and said the following, "I don't date a lot. My friends help. Actually, my friends are amazing. Anyone would want them as friends. We do all sorts of things together: picnics in the park, progressive dinners, birthday parties, bike trips, backpacking trips, camping trips. Now and then we go to a play or the ballet. Sometimes we'll visit a museum or listen to a jazz group. We go for walks at the lake. We may eat popcorn and watch a video. I enjoy my friends so much."

"Are these friends all single?"

"No, some of them are married. Several have children, but these are usually adult outings. She continued, "I miss being married. I know some people who will marry a strange guy and those of us who know her through work or socially can't believe it. Just to legalize having sex or own property? It's not worth it. We're talking about messing up my life. I like my life."

She smiled and I said, "Thanks." the conversation changed to another subject.

There can be subtle pressure on single parents from family, friends, classmates, and work associates to be married. Single people tell me they are teased and the butt of jokes and well-intentioned matchmaking. More than one has said, "As the years pass, people ask me if my standards are too high or they wonder if I'm insecure or maybe a lesbian or gay."

Some singles enjoy their freedom and privacy, but others wonder out loud if they will ever find someone with whom they can share their joys and struggles and dreams. More than a few women have said to me, "I have to live for God and care for myself. If someone comes along, that would be nice, but I can't sit around waiting."

I did not realize among early Christians, at least as it seemed in the New Testament, that the norm apparently was single. Yes, Peter the apostle had a mother-in-law and Priscilla and Aquila were married, but they appear to be exceptions. The closest followers of Jesus were single—James and John (sons of Zebedee), Andrew and Phillip, Bartholomew and Matthew, Thomas and James son of Alphaeus, Simon the Zealot and Thaddeus, Judas Iscariot, Mary Magdalene, Lazarus and Mary and Martha. Jesus himself was single.

In the early church there were Saul and Stephen, Matthias, Dorcas, Lydia, and Phoebe. Now some could have been married, but it seems strange that very few couples or spouses are mentioned.

So how can people who are single Christians deal with their sex drive? The same way I and other married people deal with our sex drives if our spouse has morning sickness or an extended illness or is out of the country. Sexual energy can be released through regular masturbation, physical exercise, chopping wood, competitive sports, dancing, swimming, or playing the piano.

Those of you who are single may reply, "But that's easy for you to say, Gary. You're married." But what if my wife's sexual needs are not the same as my own? Or she is out of town on an extended visit? I've had needs and faced temptation, but with God's help I've chosen not to act on those desires. I've noticed that sexual behavior among unmarried believers often appears to be not much different from the sexual behavior of nonbelievers. Just because it appears "everybody is doing it," does not make it right. I know there is little support in society, but I believe the Holy One wants us to love God with our bodies as well as our minds and emotions. God wants to be our first love and best love.

If you are single, you need a community of family and friends. The church may be part of that community. It's important to have someone whom you can go to a movie, have a meal, go for a run, have a good cry, or take a vacation with. In the New Testament being single is not what prevents us from being whole but from being out of touch with Christ and his community.

QUESTIONS FOR REFLECTION

- Do you think the world has lost sight of the value and art of friendship?
- How can we have opposite and same sex friends and still maintain boundaries that honor God?

PRAYER

- Jesus, love me in those deep places and make yourself one with me so that I am filled with your Spirit—that can be enough. Amen.

I am a Virgin

WHEN I FIRST HEARD Madonna sing the song, "Like a Virgin," I thought, "You are anything but a virgin!" Why is it today that being a virgin is not something either cherished or encouraged? Maybe it is because we live in a society that markets products on the basis of instant gratification. We want to know it, taste it, experience it right now. Why wait when you can enjoy intimacy now.

One evening, thirty-five of us were at a party which was part of a spiritual growth adult weekend together. People were standing around visiting and eating crackers and cheese, assorted fruit and snacks, while sampling various wines, sparkling cider, and beer. I struck up a conversation with a man I was barely acquainted with. I took a risk and shared something personal. He began to open up, and soon we were deep in conversation.

Surrounded by people, some within hearing range, he quietly said, "When I was eighteen years old I was still a virgin. I was embarrassed, however, so I lied to my buddies and bragged about my sexual exploits. I was so stupid. Then I enlisted in the military and ended up being close to the front lines of the war zone. I found myself thinking, 'I could die over here, and I've experienced so little of life. I have never been intimate with a woman.' So, I went out and did it." He wasn't specific about whether he did it with a local woman or a prostitute. It probably doesn't matter.

He continued, "Before my first wife and I were married, we lived together. Since my divorce, I've had other partners. I have been sort of sexually monogamous. I've only been sexually intimate with the person I was dating at that time. What I've discovered is that sex is a powerful experience, but it's also a spiritual experience. I've learned a lot. Surprisingly, I have not slept with my fiancée since we became engaged. We decided to wait until we were married so that on our honeymoon it will be like the first time."

"Why is that?" I asked.

"We wanted this to be special."

I wanted to clap, and cheer, and say, "Amen!" but I couldn't because of the crowd. I listened until he concluded speaking and then I said, "I am very happy for both of you!" Strange we get so smart so old.

I have a friend whose wife told me that when he was single and dating he had three criteria for the woman he would eventually marry. The first was that she be a Christian with whom he could share his faith. The second was that she enjoy music, since he was a musician. The third was that she be a virgin. He didn't say whether or not he was a virgin, but I assumed that he was. There is something special about knowing that when you have sexual intercourse, it is for the first time. Then you can learn and explore and grow together in this area as well as all the other areas of your life.

I know all this sounds quite unrealistic and idealistic given the attitudes and behavior I witness among many of our church youth, young adults, and adults. I can't help thinking that for those who decide not to be sexually intimate until marriage, God will bless them with pleasure, joy, and freedom that makes the waiting worthwhile. That has certainly been true in our case as a couple. Each decade has brought change, challenge, and creativity. What used to be pleasurable may change.

Baptized into Christ Jesus even though we may have lost our virginity before marriage, we can be forgiven. I believe it is important to ask. God sees us as pure. Non-virgins can return to practicing chastity after they crossed the line.

QUESTIONS FOR REFLECTION

- If you lost your virginity before marriage, how does God's acceptance make you feel?

- If you had it to do over again, would you do anything differently?

PRAYER

- Holy One, help us to save ourselves for the right person and then "to shoot the works" when we make a commitment for life. Amen.

Finding a Mate

I HAD DAMAGED AN aging ligament on the inside of my knee through overexercising and a pair of worn out shoes. My family physician informed me that while I did not need surgery, I should see a physical therapist. During my first visit to a physical therapist I was assigned to a woman named Beth. She told me that my mental attitude could help coupled with powerful massage, electrical stimulation of the nerves, and a variety of exercises.

While she began to push and pull my leg while I was lying on my side on a bench, I decided to learn more about her. "How did you get into physical therapy?" I asked.

"In college I took a lot of classes in science," she answered. "My father wanted me to be a doctor, but since we didn't get along, I rebelled. I didn't want to dedicate such a large portion of my time and life to preparing for something that takes as long to prepare for as becoming a doctor. I still wanted to serve people, so I chose physical therapy."

I continued to ask questions and inquired what she enjoyed about her profession, what was difficult about her profession, and how she saw it changing in the future. She asked me what I did. I gave her a brief biography on my marriage, family, and work.

It seemed natural for me to ask, "Are you married?" She replied, "Oh, I've been married about three months." By this time, I was really feeling relaxed. "Can you tell me about this lucky guy?"

"He's a carpenter."

"How did you meet him?" I asked.

"I advertised. I had seen ads in the local weeklies as well as on television for singles desiring a relationship or mate."

"Really?"

"I wrote an ad for the personals in the *Seattle Post-Intelligencer* and the *Seattle Times*."

"Do you mind my asking what you said?" I was genuinely curious.

"Not at all," she continued. "I am single, female, and in my thirties. I am interested in a long-term relationship and I have never been married. I enjoy the outdoors, dancing, and classical music. Height must not be a problem for you since I am quite tall." Beth is large-boned and I would guess her to be probably 6'4".

My curiosity got the better of me. "Did you get many respondents?"

"Forty-five," Beth replied.

"Wow, how did you screen the candidates?"

"Most of them sent a photo and a letter indicating their age, employment, education, interests, and expectations. I eliminated the majority by their initial response and wrote them a note expressing my gratitude for their inquiry and the fact that I was not interested in pursuing it any further. I did date several, and one date was enough for me to know they weren't my type."

"How far down the list was Chuck?"

"He must have been forty-three or forty-four. I almost didn't contact the last few because I was getting discouraged."

"What happened?"

"Well, we went out on a date for dinner and dancing. It was so good we planned a second date." Then Beth said something quite amazing, "I thought to myself, 'I do not know what it feels like to be loved. I am not sure whether he is the right one. All I know is that I have never felt more respected, valued, and cared for with anyone I've been with.' I didn't want to lose him."

"So, what happened?"

"I asked him to marry me."

"You asked after two dates?"

"Yep, and he said yes. He moved up here and we got married two months later."

"That's some story."

"He's quite a guy."

I lay there quietly while she manipulated my leg and thought about what she had said. There are similarities between getting to know God and getting to know a potential mate. We do not know what God's love feels like, but if we let God love us, and we begin to experience that love, we don't want to lose it. Faith involves risking and trusting that what we see and hear and experience of God's love is the real thing.

How we find our life partners is somewhat of a mystery to me. A former parishioner once said to me when we were discussing how some people are attracted to one another, "Gary, I've never figured out why a particular horse fly lands on a particular horse apple." He was from Montana but I think the analogy still fits. Once we leave school, it may seem harder to make contact; people tell me it is more difficult to find a date. Our work, the church, an athletic team, an interest group, a political caucus, a neighborhood or school association, a bookstore, coffee shop, vacation tour, fellow bus rider, family, or friends can all be possible sources for finding who's out there and available.

Once you find them, what criteria do you use for screening? I believe the input of family and friends is invaluable. When we meet someone we may marry, we are marrying the person's family, too. An urban hospital chaplain once said to a group of us, "The boy becomes the man he lives with. It is important to find out how he feels concerning his father. When it's possible, I'd say meet his father or whoever was the primary male figure in his childhood and adolescence. It might be a step-father or a grandfather or uncle. Is this person friendly, loving, truthful, interesting? Do you feel safe around him? Do you like the way he relates to his wife, parents, children, or other family members? The man you're considering will become like his father in forty years," the chaplain said.

"But what if the man you're dating didn't have a father, or had a negative experience, or a series of men who were not healthy models as provider, parent, nurturer, spiritual teacher, and warrior?" the chaplain asked. He said, "I would be very nervous."

The chaplain also said, "The girl becomes the woman she lives with." So, it is important to find out how she feels about her mother or step-mother or grandmother or aunt. Where it's possible, I'd say meet her mother or the primary female figure in her childhood and adolescence. Is this person friendly, loving, truthful, interesting? Do you feel comfortable around her? Do you like the way she relates to her husband, parents, children or other family members? The person you're dating will become like her mother in forty years. But what if the woman you're dating didn't have a mother to raise her, or had a negative experience, or had whole series of women who weren't healthy models in terms of being a provider, parent, nurturer, spiritual teacher, and protector? I'd be very nervous.

I would also be cautious choosing someone from a broken family to be my spouse. However, I realize with hard work, God's help, and the support of others, people can rise above unfortunate beginnings.

I prayed for a life partner and believe I was guided to God's choice for my life. I could have married another woman, but I am forever grateful that when I wasn't sure what it felt like to be loved, I listened for God's guidance.

QUESTIONS FOR REFLECTION

- How will you know when you've met the right person?
- If you're married, was your choice more than dumb luck?

PRAYER

- Our Father, it's truly a mystery in all the millions of people to find the one with whom I can make a commitment for life. If I have found someone, thanks. If I haven't, be the center of my life so I don't blow it. Amen.

We're a Couple,
but We Are Not Married

WHILE ATTENDING A CLERGY gathering in Seattle, I phoned a friend whom we've known for twenty-four years. Often, we'll call each other once or twice a year. In our conversation, I said, "Tell me about the children." He answered, "Our oldest, Kyle, is out on his own and working in construction. Cleo is attending Pacific Lutheran University and still struggling with identity issues, and Evan, who's the middle one, is still going to school but fallen in lust."

"That's a descriptive expression," I said.

Wyatt chuckled and said, "Evan has moved in with his girlfriend. They've dated for several years. We like her. They will probably get married when he finishes school."

I found myself thinking, "Why can't they get married while they are still in school?" but I was respectful and didn't ask. Besides, at this point, Wyatt and his wife have no control.

The State of Oregon has passed a Domestic Partners Law to protect the rights of unmarried heterosexual and gay or lesbian partners in long-term relationships. To me this represented a significant societal shift from the traditional norm of marriage. It is partly a result of lobbying and litigation by special interest groups, but it is a concession to a societal shift. In my childhood people spoke of single adults cohabiting as a "common-law marriage." Now we simply speak of them as "a couple" and everyone understands. Lots of Christian young adults I know are "couples," sometimes on the sly from their parents, but just as many don't care what other people think. I've heard many parents grieve and say, "That's not the way we raised her. I don't know what's gotten into her," or "We never would have guessed our son would end up doing this. It's as though he's turned his back on our values and the teaching of the church."

A woman I know says, "Living together is like 'playing house.' I've told my girls if somebody wants your body, make them give you his name as well. Don't pretend it's real when it's not. Sharing expenses, meals, and a bed does not make you married."

Rarely as a pastor do I see couples who are living together break up and do it cheerfully. Usually one party has made a stronger commitment and ends up deeply hurt. Each time it happens, they lose a little more of themselves. Eventually they may get to the point where they no longer trust their own choices in relationships and end up with anxiety attacks or depression. Living together with kids can send mixed signals. It messes kids up too.

Couples have told me there are different reasons why people live together. "We want to see if we're compatible. We know a lot of people who got married and later got a divorce." Other people have told me, "I wanted to see if I was sexually fulfilled. In my first marriage I did all the initiating and she tolerated it." Still others have said, "We're living together because it's cheaper." The age range on that one is twenties to mid-eighties. Some couples were sexually intimate and found it to be hard to live apart, so they moved in with each other. And some people have said to me, "I was betrayed and hurt the first time around. I won't let that happen again." Behind the words I sense a fear of commitment.

David and Linda have lived together since she was in college. Her folks went through a divorce and she is not close to her mother. She hinted, whined, prayed, and tried to cajole David into marriage, but he kept weaseling out on her. He's been in the military service and worked abroad. She's waited for him or gone along. The last time I saw them their roles had flipped. He wanted to get married and she was giving him the run-around. Now they are back in the area and they're still not married after seven or eight years. It must take a lot of energy to keep such an important relationship on such an erratic basis.

A mother, homemaker, teacher, and nurse said one Sunday morning in a Bible study, "When we're watching television and we see values portrayed that are contrary to our faith and family, I tell our children, 'They didn't get it right. The order is love, marriage, sex, and children.'" She'd probably agree that friendship comes before love. She and I both know that her teaching is counter-cultural. The movies and television portray the most frequent order as "sex, love, maybe marriage, rarely children." The majority of couples I marry are living together regardless of their age. The sad truth is that you cannot know what it's like to be married until you make the commitment to be married before God and others. Living together by its very nature is temporary.

QUESTIONS FOR REFLECTION

- Why does lust tend to win out over keeping faith?
- What might move you or a couple who is living together toward a commitment to marriage?

PRAYER

- You are the Way. When people don't know they're loved, they don't seem to know how to love. Help each of us to experience your love personally so that, loving ourselves, we can learn to love each other as you intended. Amen.

Is Engagement Outmoded?

Renee lived with her dog and two cats when we first met. Thirty-something, I would describe her as independent, creative, and somewhat reclusive. Self-employed and seemingly self-sufficient, she yearned to be married. Well-read and deeply cultured, she played the violin, piano, and flute. She also enjoyed the wilderness and lived in a small cabin on some forested acreage.

As a teenager she did some dating but often under a watchful parental eye. While in college she had a steady boyfriend. After she graduated, they kept in touch, but she wasn't ready for marriage. She struggled with a lot of "what-ifs." "What if we marry and I find out he's not what I thought he was? What if he only pretended to believe in God because he knows that's important to me? What if we're not sexually compatible? What if we got married and it doesn't work out and we have to get a divorce? I don't believe in divorce." So, Renee cooled the relationship. Years later, he tracked her down and phoned her, but she was hesitant. That was the last she heard of him and she's kicked herself ever since. "Gary, I think I missed my chance," she said later one afternoon, her eyes brimming with tears.

Men were attracted to her in subsequent years, but she said they were mostly agnostics and atheists. They ran the gamut of occupations, but few had a personal faith or were interested in the church. There were months when she struggled with depression at the thought of spending the rest of her life alone. I thought of her periodically and would find myself hoping and praying that someone would find her and appreciate exactly how unique she was and not spook her away.

Every now and then she would appear in worship on Sunday with a man. We would visit and she would introduce him as a friend or acquaintance. I would never see any of the men a second time. One Sunday she brought a man and a woman. Somehow, I got the idea that the newcomers were a couple, but that proved not to be the case.

"They're just friends," Renee said. In the ensuing weeks the man returned with Renee to worship. I visited with him and began to get to know him somewhat. He was several years older than Renee and had been single all his life as well. Although he was raised Christian, he was currently not practicing. It soon became apparent that Carl was pretty serious about Renee. She tended to downplay the romance, but I could tell she was pleased and interested, too. Slowly she began to bring Carl to classes, church potlucks, and choir concerts. She began to ask her Christian friends what they thought of him.

Then I didn't see them for several months, so I wrote her a note. She called to apologize and say things had gotten pretty serious. They were thinking about getting married and wondered if I would do some pre-marriage counseling. I replied in the affirmative. We set a time and they came in for our first meeting. We jumped right into serious conversation. We discussed money and sex, communication and conflict, families of origin and children, values and religion.

During our third session, Renee mentioned that they were going to another state to work for the summer. While they'd live in the same apartment, they would each have separate bedrooms. She told me, "We want to do things right and don't want to be sexual until after we are married. Carl agrees to this and respects me."

I told them that they were much stronger in their resolve than I would have been at their age. I said to them, "You two are pretty unusual."

She laughed and said, "Being this close will either cement us or cure us."

The two of them moved east to work together for about five months. We kept in touch through the mail. She wrote how Carl was interested in learning more about God. They read from the Bible each day and discussed it. She was thrilled that he was interested in God and sincerely receptive. She indicated that the two of them had little in common with most of the people they worked with, who she said were "not interested in spiritual things. They assume we're sleeping together because we share the same apartment. It's hard not to be, so keep us in your prayers." I assured them I would.

When they returned to the city I was living in, they shared with me how they had grown, relied on each other, and become good friends. They also said they would be going to his family's town to work and be married the end of that summer. I was delighted for both of them and told them I was glad they had taken some time to explore their relationship. I called to wish them well the week of their wedding.

I was not able to go back for the celebration but stopped to visit when they returned to the area. They showed me the home they were building together. They were living in a garage temporarily and things were a bit crowded. She put the teapot on and we visited for a while.

"How's it going?" I asked.

"Great," he said. She nodded. When he stepped out for a few minutes, she whispered quietly, "It's harder than I thought it would be."

"It is hard," I said to her. "I can't imagine anything harder than for two people so different to make a commitment to spend their lives together." She nodded somberly. I thought of all the trials and tears in my first year of marriage. "You two have taken the time to lay a foundation for your marriage. You've involved family and friends. It's a lot of work. With God's help you'll make it."

"Do you think so?" she asked as I was getting up to leave.

"Yes. God wants it to work, too."

Even though Renee's first few months were hard, she and her husband benefitted from the soul searching and exploration they invested during their engagement. An engagement is an opportunity to explore, receive feedback from others, and ask God's guidance.

QUESTIONS FOR REFLECTION

- Why do you think so many people today bypass a formal engagement time prior to their marriage?
- If a friend contemplating marriage were to ask you the benefits and tasks of an engagement period, how would you respond?

PRAYER

- Covenanting God, may any of your people who are contemplating marriage allow themselves the time to explore and test their relationship before saying "I do." Amen.

Abstinence Is an Option

I usually co-teach at a high school confirmation class. This is a time when youth study the beliefs of the Christian church, publicly profess their faith in the Triune God, and covenant to identify with the life and mission of the adult Christian community. In preparing for a retreat on the Ten Commandments, my fellow teacher and I divided up responsibility for presenting the various commandments. One of those which she selected was the sixth commandment, "You shall not commit adultery." As part of her preparation, she interviewed a seventeen-year-old neighbor girl and asked the following questions: "What are your views on having sexual relations before marriage? Does your faith influence your behavior on dates? Are your friends sexually active or abstinent?"

The girl told Teena how she was asked to a dance by a popular boy who happened to be a good student, good looking, and had lettered in three sports. They had a delightful evening and soon they began to date. Early on the boy started to make moves on her, and kissing moved to petting, petting moved to heavy petting with pressure to go all the way. The girl said no. The boy persisted, but she held firm. He told her it was stupid and that "everybody's doing it." She broke up with him and she was ostracized by his friends as word got around. Teena asked her why she refused. The girl replied, "My body belongs to God and I want to save myself for the person I will spend my life with."

I was impressed with both her clear thinking and her resolve. She represents a minority worth encouraging. She went on to indicate many of her classmates were sexually active.

"Why do you think they are?" Teena asked.

"Because they don't have a strong enough self-image and need to be needed, or they want to enjoy the experience and feel safe because of birth control."

What if you're older, you've dated, are in love, and plan to be married anyway? What's wrong with sleeping together then? Lots of people do, even Christians. A psychiatric nurse told me that "intercourse is conversation at the most intimate level. It involves the mind, emotions, body, and spirit. You cannot give yourself safely and freely outside the covenant of marriage without risking great loss."

I agree. Let's say someone you care about—a sibling, a child, a grandchild, or a parent—is sexually active with someone you or they deeply care about. If for some reason the relationship doesn't work out, it can be a devastating betrayal because the person you care about has given themselves totally and the other person walked away. Whether they admit it or not, they've lost a part of themselves. Each time it happens again they will lose a little bit more of themselves. If it happens enough times, a person can end up totally disillusioned and disdainful of believing commitment is possible.

A dear friend of mine sought to faithfully love his spouse for many years. Publicly everything looked great, but privately it was a sham. His wife was critical, controlling, and sexually unresponsive. They only had sex to conceive their three children. She buried herself in her job and professional organizations. After years of verbal abuse and neglect, he finally said, "I can no longer live this lie." Many people were saddened by the divorce. All but his closest friends knew only one side. Eventually he learned his wife was living with another woman. He was saddened but had suspected she might be lesbian or bisexual.

Years of pent-up anger erupted into rage. Whenever he was near her, he would get hooked and just unravel. There followed several years of therapy and slowly he began to heal. He began to consider the possibility of dating. Four years after the divorce he began dating. He was very cautious, and if someone pressed he backed off. Then he met a woman who was divorced. She was good with his children. Slowly but surely he began to trust. He had wondered if he ever could again. He started to relax and let his guard down. They laughed and played together over the next several weeks. She complimented him and encouraged him. They spent more time together. They became engaged. Hesitating and a bit tearfully, they agreed to make love. They told his children and her children. They said their prayers and melted together after a romantic evening out. He later told me it felt wonderful to be held, to give and receive love, after having been deeply hurt. They both had eyes only for each other.

Gradually, things turned sour. The relationship began to show signs of strain and stress. There were sharp words, long silences, tears, and outbursts. She became critical of his children. His old fears of rejection resurfaced, and eventually they broke up. He told me that it was painful for both of them. He knew now he was not impotent. Still, ending their relationship was like a wrenching tear in the fabric of both of their beings.

The break-up also caused grief among family and friends who had cared for them but who didn't know how intimate the relationship had become, nor how it deteriorated.

The church has taught that God created the gift of sexual intercourse for within a marriage alone. I believe this is a safeguard for the couple, the children, the family, the church, and the larger community. We can rationalize not marrying and still having intercourse, but we do it to our own peril. Every Christian I have talked to who had sexual intercourse before marriage has told me they would wait if they had the opportunity to do things over again.

Even after marriage there may be times for abstinence due to pregnancy, illness, childbirth, geographic separation, sexual drive, stress, or exhaustion. We may not be able to have sex. We may have to wait. With the help of God's Spirit, we can control our desires.

When the time is right, it can be so delicious that the waiting is forgotten.

QUESTIONS FOR REFLECTION

- Why has abstinence not been encouraged more publicly for our youth, singles, the divorced, and the widowed?
- If you are single and haven't practiced sexual abstinence, would there be a value in beginning to right now?

PRAYER

- God, you are the source and you have promised to unite all in your love. Guide our thoughts and actions, that in matters of sex we may honor you, not cheat ourselves, nor mute the witness of the Gospel in the world. Amen.

I Believe in Public Sex

DURING A PREACHING WORKSHOP at the University of Victoria one of the two keynoters, who is an ethicist, said, "I believe in public sex."

Some of the registrants chuckled, but others gasped. He wasn't affirming what a parish council president of a congregation I served in Portland saw in his office parking lot—a prostitute doing it with a John while leaning against a building.

Stanley said it one more time as if to either shock us or provoke our thinking. "I believe in public sex, not private sex. Jesus quoting Genesis said, 'For this reason a man shall leave his father and mother and be joined to his wife and the two shall become one flesh.' Presumably a woman shall leave her father and mother and be joined to her husband and the two shall become one flesh as well." Stanley beamed. "That's public sex. The appropriate setting for sexual intercourse is marriage, where it's protected within a lifelong commitment which is celebrated in a public rite. Marriage is not a private affair."

The popular cultural belief is that what two consenting adults do in the privacy of their living room, shower, or bedroom is their own business. This is contrary to the church's understanding of Scripture. What one member of the body of Christ does, affects the other members of the body. All our personal words and actions weaken or strengthen the life and witness of Christ's body, the church.

Marriage is like a three-legged stool. One leg is the Creator, since love is God's idea. One leg is the community of family, friends, and faith. And one leg is the couple. If we were to remove the leg of the community the marriage would be weak. No two people can completely meet each other's needs. They need a larger community of people who can serve as a support network, a sounding board, a guiding light, and a buffer, as well as providing wisdom figures who can be models and mentors. If we remove the leg of the Creator in the marriage it will be less stable and there is a good chance it will collapse. The couple also needs God. Our personal relationship with God is always the primary one. God's love is the source of self-love and the glue of human love. From the Spirit of God flow the gifts of forgiveness, patience, kindness, gentleness, unity, humor, play, and prayer.

Jesus said to his followers, "A new commandment I give you. That you love one another as I have loved you." He washed the disciples' feet. Jesus' love is the servant's love. Living in him, husband and wife look for ways to wait on each other. Service is not always convenient or glamorous. Jesus' love is a self-emptying love. We see it on the cross, "The good shepherd laying down his life for the sheep." We experience it in the Eucharist, "Take and eat, this is my body broken for you." In Christ we don't hold back but we learn to give our whole self unreservedly to our partner. Jesus' love is a unitive love. In the Gospel of John Jesus said, "I pray that they may be one Father even as we are one, I in them and you in me, that they may become completely one, so that the world may know you have sent me and loved them even as you love me." In Christ Jesus we are to image God's love to one another. The union of that love can be a witness of something new to others.

Love by itself is not the only reason for marriage. I like to ask two questions of couples who come to me during preparation for marriage as well as those who come for enrichment in a marriage care class I teach. They are as follows:

First, "Will this person enhance your relationship with God?" Or, "Has this person enhanced your relationship with God?"

If the answer is yes, that's great. If the answer is no, pay attention, because God wants to be our first love.

Second, "Will this person enable you to live out your faith as a follower of Jesus in daily life?" Or, "Has this person enabled you to live out your faith as a follower of Jesus in daily life?"

If the answer is yes, well and good. If the answer is no, pay attention since "you cannot serve two masters."

Each of us is called to reflect God's love in Christ to our spouse to nourish and heal them and empower them for their ministry in the world.

Most marriages go through several stages: beginning the marriage, pursuing a career, bearing children if you choose, mid-life, pre-retirement, retirement, aging, and preparing for death. God wants to be the wellspring for all those stages and the changes and challenges each stage brings. The divine plan is that sex, like marriage, always occurs within the context and love of the Creator and a community. I believe to ignore this is to shortchange ourselves.

QUESTIONS FOR REFLECTION

- Has Christ's presence made a difference in how you love your spouse?

- Are there one or two ways you would like to love your spouse with God's help?

PRAYER

- God, you are both one and a community. Help me to love my spouse the way Christ loves the church. Amen.

Coming Out

IN 1988 THE SECRETARY'S memo said, "Call Carol," and I did. Initially I received an answering machine, so I left a message. We played phone tag the next three or four days but eventually we made contact. Carol began by saying, "We haven't talked for a long time and I wanted to check in with you, Pastor Gary."

"I would like to catch up with you, too," I replied. We agreed on one o'clock Thursday at a local restaurant.

Carol had, to my knowledge, never been married. Somewhat shy with a warm smile, she had a cute sense of humor. I sensed in previous visits she struggled with self-esteem and family of origin issues. She grew up in a Christian home but has always been on the edge of the church as long as I've known her. She worshipped periodically but had chosen not to join the congregation I was serving. Occasionally I would see her at a congregational function, but she had come and gone through the years.

It was a lovely spring day as the two of us visited together under a sun umbrella at an outdoor table. We caught up on her work, her family, her latest move, and her plans for the summer. Then she said, "There is something I'd like to talk about, only it's kind of awkward."

"Nothing will make me think less of you. I've probably heard something similar, so it won't shock me."

"I've met somebody," she said.

"Can you tell me about the person?"

"I've never really dated much. In high school I went to dances and drive-in movies with a few guys, but it was so-so. Through the years I have never really clicked with anybody. As I've gotten older, I wondered whether it was just me and whether I'd ever find someone." I nodded. "I'm not very attractive and often feel awkward in social situations." I listened. "Well, I've met someone I really like only she is a woman." She grimaced and waited for my response.

"I'd like to hear about her."

Hesitantly, she continued. "She works upstairs from me at the plant and we met and visited over lunch. She's fun to be with, stimulating in conversation, and I find myself being attracted to her." She looked at me again, waiting for my response, and I nodded. "I find myself being excited when I'm with her. I leave work and feel like a kid. I'm so happy I want to skip all the way home to my apartment." I smiled at the thought of her skipping. "I go around humming and that's not like me. I look forward to seeing her. Do you think I am a lesbian?"

"Being attracted to someone of the same sex doesn't necessarily make a person a lesbian. But it may be possible. Ask God to guide you."

"But I've never felt quite like this toward anybody." I was inwardly pleased for her. "What does the church say about this?"

I talked with her about our denomination's initial draft on human sexuality and the subsequent revisions. I told her it had generated a lot of heated debate, particularly around certain issues—one of them being gay/lesbian relationships. I told her how theologians, bishops, pastors, and parishioners have different perspectives on the subject. We discussed the difference between sexual orientation and sexual behavior.

"What would the people at your CTS congregation think?" she asked.

"Some would say it wasn't a problem. Others would say it's not scriptural but they would still be accepting of the person. And others would say it's sinful and should not be tolerated. A few parents might be fearful of the message this might send to their children or youth."

"Are there any gays or lesbians at CTS?"

"Yes," I replied.

"Are they out in the open?"

"They are only with trusted friends."

"Have you had any same-sex couples in the congregation?"

"We have but they have moved on or split up."

"How did people respond to them?"

"Some of their friends were accepting, but some felt it wasn't right. Others knew both parties and felt they were good people."

"What about you, Pastor G? What do you think?"

I silently said a prayer, swallowed deeply, and began my answer. "I have read everything I can get my hands on about this subject by various authors of different denominations, gay and straight. I had questions about whether the church's stand is correct. I feel uncomfortable ignoring over three thousand years of Judeo-Christian teaching and practice on this subject."

"There is a problem," Carol interrupted.

"Oh?" I gave her a quizzical look.

"This woman is troubled by the fact that I'm a Christian."

"Why is that?"

"She has been in relationships with other women. One was a Christian and it was tough. As a matter of fact, she recently ended a relationship that was hurtful, so she's wary. She is also bothered by the fact that I have no experience."

"You mean she is bothered because you're a virgin?"

"Yes. It hurts me since my faith is deep and part of who I am. It also makes me sad since I've never been into sleeping around casually."

"That would bother me too, Carol." I replied. "God wants to be our first love. We often want to occupy God's place. When we begin to experience God's love, Scripture teaches that we can begin to love ourselves and others rightly and faithfully. If this woman is implying she must come before God in your life, that would make me uneasy."

"It makes me uneasy, too, but I'm still attracted to her and think about her a lot."

We spoke a little longer. It was an honest, loving, heart to heart conversation.

"Carol, not all the data is in yet on sexual orientation and whether it's environmental and involves learned behavior or whether it's biochemical and simply part of who we are as persons. More research needs to be done. My own observation is that most gay/lesbian people I know would not consciously choose homosexuality given the costs in terms of typical family fallout and prejudice at work, school, and in congregational life. Often there is just too much pain." I told Carol that I was continuing to learn and the church had wrestled with this too.

"But what if orientation is a given as the evidence suggests? What if I am who I am because that's how I was created? I'm created in the image of God. I'm baptized. I love Jesus. I want to serve him. It just so happens I'm attracted to someone of the same gender. I don't want to be promiscuous. I'm not a pedophile. If I found someone and we wanted to make a life commitment, would you do a blessing?"

"I would welcome you and your partner. The church I'm a part of has said that our Scriptures teach that marriage is between a man and a woman and has not authorized blessing couples of the same gender who want to be life partners. I don't want to ignore that church, but I'm willing to challenge the tradition."

As our conversation was concluding I thanked Carol for trusting me. I told her she might talk to other clergy to hear their wisdom. I reaffirmed my appreciation for her as a person, a woman of faith, and a child of God. She said, "Thank you, Gary. I knew I could trust you. It's been helpful. Can we talk again?"

"You bet."

She beamed and gave me a hug. After she left, I felt miserable. Many members of the Evangelical Lutheran Church and other Christian denominations have changed their minds as they have learned more about sexual orientation. I know I have grown through conversations with gay and lesbian Christians who have been patient with me.

I remember a physician, David, who was speaking on homosexuality in 1996 at a retreat center about stories of gay and lesbian Christians. He asked, "How many of you know what Jesus said about homosexuality?" He waited. People had puzzled expressions on their faces.

"Not one word. Jesus said, 'From the beginning, God created us male and female and said . . . the two shall become one flesh.'" David continued to argue that the Scriptures speak against incest, rape, promiscuity, prostitution, and pedophilia but seem to know nothing of same sex believers in loving, faithful, mutually serving, lifelong, committed relationships. Since the Scriptures are normative within my tradition, I have thought about his remarks often.

QUESTIONS FOR REFLECTION

- Do you have a gay or lesbian family member?

- Would your relationship or regard for someone you know well change if they told you that they were lesbian or gay? On what basis would it change?

- If they asked you for spiritual guidance, to what resources would you turn besides your own personal beliefs and experiences?

PRAYER

- God of the universe, help me to do that which pleases you and to be gracious and respectful and learn from each person. Amen.

Marriage Equality

THE COMPACT TRUCK PULLED up as I was driving along the river front in downtown Portland, Oregon. In the front seat two women sat laughing and talking. In the rear window of the cab was a sticker that said, "Against Initiative 609 and 610. Say No to Hate Crimes." The two bills were defeated last year in Washington but a new one would be on the state ballot in November of 2014 exclaiming "Equal Rights Not Special Rights." The judgmental attitude of some of the religious right makes me uneasy. On the rear bumper was another bumper sticker that said, "We are everywhere like aliens, stamp collectors, and Basset hounds. Honor Diversity." Wisdom is where you find it!

The Holy Spirit works in the church, but also in the world. I believe one sign of that is the societal recognition that sexual orientation is something that we are born with. Our sexual orientation is part of who we are. Same sex couples are more visible now. They have the same needs, struggles, and dreams as heterosexual couples. I see them visiting and sometimes joining Christian congregations. There has been more listening, conversation, and sharing of stories since I had that conversation with Carol in 1988. We need to start with who people are and not just their sexual orientation.

There has been more movement and acceptance in some mainline denominations rather than others. A growing number of congregations have signed a charter to be Reconciled in Christ congregations. Signing this charter means "all people are welcomed, regardless of ethnicity, race, ability, gender, sexual orientation, or age." Some congregations have a Reconciling in Christ committee which educates, advocates, and supports LGBTQ people, couples, and families.

One of the questions I have asked congregations is, "If your son, daughter, or grandchild were gay, how would you want congregation members to treat them?" The good news is that God creates, loves, and welcomes all people.

Some denominations have written and authorized same-sex marriage liturgies. The Supreme Court has legalized same-sex marriage. Some denominations have ordained gay and lesbian seminarians as pastors after they've been trained, approved, and called to serve a congregation.

Sara and Mary are both Christian pastors. One serves a Lutheran congregation and one serves an Episcopal congregation. They met, got to know each other professionally, dated, and had the support of their parents and siblings. They spoke with their denominational executives and decided to get married. I went to their wedding in 2012. There were about six hundred guests. Lutheran and Episcopal bishops presided. The music was inspiring. The liturgy and homily were well-done. At the conclusion of the service, Sara and Mary were introduced as a married couple. Guests clapped, whistled, and cheered. The newlyweds' faces were full of smiles and tears of joy. The reception was playful with good food, laughter, and a jazz band. I was blessed as a participant, and happy that the State and the church, under the influence of the Spirit, made this possible. People on the street asked about the joyful celebration. I explained and told them it was an historic event. Many of them said they were supportive.

We've grown as a church, but there is still fear, prejudice, and wounding that occurs in some denominations, congregations, and families. I'm hopeful that Christians who have changed their minds will stand in solidarity with their LGBTQ sisters and brothers.

QUESTIONS FOR REFLECTION

- Has your experience with gay, lesbian, bisexual, or transgender people of faith changed your understanding and views?
- Have LGBTQ members enriched a congregation you've been a part of? How?

PRAYER

- God, forgive us for being so slow to embrace and welcome our LGBTQ sisters and brothers as members of your church. Thank you for the patience and love our LGBTQ sisters and brothers have extended to those of us who are "straight." Amen.

Romance after Marriage

ONE SUMMER I ATTENDED an Institute on Peace in the Americas. I was gone for three weeks. Gail and I had not been separated for that long since I was in graduate school. The time away was intellectually challenging and politically an eye opener as I listened to various Christians and church leaders from different parts of Central and South America speak each morning on the political and economic injustices they were subject to. In the afternoons I was taking a class in conversational Spanish, "Espanol Rapido." But I still missed my wife.

My return flight got me into Bellingham around eight in the evening and Gail was waiting for me at the airport. She greeted me and we embraced. It was good to be in my hometown and good to be together. I was tired and ready to head home. A shower sounded good after twelve hours in planes and airports. I put my head back and closed my eyes while she drove.

The car stopped and I opened my eyes, thinking we were home. "Why are we here?" I asked as I lifted my head and looked around at what appeared to be a commercial parking lot.

"I wanted to make one stop before we go to our house; I have a surprise for you." Gail hopped out of the car and was gone several minutes and I closed my eyes again. She opened my car door and said, "Come with me."

"Do I need anything?"

"No." We were at a motel.

I followed her up the stairs in a semi-conscious, foggy state, trying to figure out what was going on. Was it some sort of party to celebrate my homecoming? Were old friends from out of town passing through and wanting to visit? She took a key and opened the door to an empty room. She was smiling as I asked, "What's going on?"

She answered, "I knew if I brought you home, you'd check in with each of the children and I wanted you for myself, so we are staying here for the night."

"Really?"

"Yes, so make yourself comfortable. Shower if you like. I'll bring up your luggage." By the time I had taken a shower and shaved, she had brought up the luggage. On the night table stand was a grocery bag. I looked inside to find all my favorite snacks— dried apricots, trail mix, fresh fruit, Fritos, and homemade chocolate chip cookies.

"Wow," I said. We snacked and visited with no interruptions. Then we crawled into bed and made wonderful, delicious, passionate love and fell asleep in each other's arms. After twenty-eight years of marriage, my wife had kidnapped me. Just so we could be alone to talk and listen, snuggle and hold each other in our arms. I remember feeling surprised, pleased, and honored.

The next morning was taken at a leisurely pace. We went out for breakfast at a restaurant we both enjoy. We got back to the house around noon and all too quickly I fell into the old daily habits and routines.

I recall that when we lived in Missoula I gathered with a group of clergy and a Jewish psychiatrist named Dr. K every two weeks. One of the things Dr. K used to say was, "Men know how to be naturally passionate. Women, on the other hand, need to teach them how to be romantic, tender, and affectionate. What happens in the marriage bed is colored by everything a couple says, does, or experiences that day or week."

Why do so many couples tend to lose romance the longer they are married? What happens to the love notes, surprise gifts, dinner by candlelight, fresh roses, a regular date night or a weekend away, or an overnight in another city? What makes couples begin to take each other for granted instead of extending themselves for their spouses? I believe we can get bogged down in our careers and children or caring for parents and neglect the marriage.

I'm always pleased when I see an older couple holding hands, or a middle-aged couple having fun dancing closely, or a younger couple smooching on or under a beach blanket, disinterested in public opinion. Song of Songs in the Hebrew Scriptures is an erotic poem about a lover and her beloved. They delight in one another. They anticipate being together. The tender language and sensual images remind me to be more romantic and less complacent. The author suggests that the way we love our beloved is the way God loves us, and yes, even so much more.

QUESTIONS FOR REFLECTION

- Are you still romantic with your partner?
- Are there any ways you could surprise your partner to fan the flame of romance?

PRAYER

- Wooer of all creatures, help me to look for little ways and grand ways to privately and physically romance the one I've chosen to spend my days with. Amen.

Making a Baby is Easy Sometimes

EARL WAS RETIRED AND in his early seventies. He had worked as a laborer and his lanky frame was still fairly robust. His hands were like the paws of a bear, but he had a gentle demeanor. He was helpful, hardy, and there were very few things he could not fix or at least make a good attempt to repair. He and his wife lived in the same little bungalow for over forty years.

A young couple purchased the house next door to Earl and Lilly. Earl loaned them tools as needed and would help them with repairs when asked. They visited back and forth over the fence, occasionally borrowed an egg, and watched each other's homes when they went out of town.

One day Miriam came over while Earl was waxing the car in the garage.

"I have a favor to ask."

"Hi Miriam, shoot," he replied.

"Ed and I have been trying to start a family for three years." Earl kept his eyes on her face, wondering where this conversation was going. "We both hold you in the highest regard and were wondering if you would consider being the father."

"What?" Earl exclaimed, totally caught off guard by the request.

"If you would donate some of your sperm to fertilize one of my eggs, we could be parents," Miriam continued. "You and Lilly could be the grandparents. I'm a practicing Roman Catholic, so we would want to do this quietly if you are willing."

Earl laughed and said, "You really do flatter me, you know. But I've been all dried up for years."

"There's probably still something in there waiting to be used," Miriam said.

Earl laughed and said, "Sorry."

I thought of God coming to Abraham in his old age when Earl told me this story.

Later Earl told his wife about Miriam's proposal. Lilly was both defensive and offended. "Who does she think she is? Does she want you to put your sperm in a glass and then she'll . . ."

"Hey, don't fret," Earl told her.

"I always thought they were a kind of strange pair." He said "You have nothing to worry about."

"Making a baby isn't as easy as it sounds." Most of us don't think about how true that statement is for many couples.

Clark and Dorothy married in mid-life. He was a consultant, a rugged Marlboro-type man in his early forties who had never been married. Clark was a hardy man with an easygoing manner not unlike Earl's. Dorothy was nearly forty and an office manager. She was athletic and loved the outdoors. She had been married before, but that marriage had ended in divorce as a result of alcoholism and abuse. Friends of the couple were pleased they had found each other and had started dating.

They married after a brief courtship and started trying to conceive a child shortly thereafter. Dorothy had always wanted a family and knew that her biological clock was ticking. She was anxious to become pregnant as soon as possible. The weeks turned into months and nothing happened. They spoke to an OB/GYN to determine the optimum time to conceive and kept trying but had no good news to report. After nearly a year passed, Dorothy began taking hormone pills to increase the chances of her fertility and egg production.

Having had no luck, Clark and Dorothy decided to speak with a fertility specialist. While they did discuss adoption, they heard stories from older couples who had adopted only to discover that the child had special needs as a result of abuse, fetal alcohol syndrome, or a detached personality. They decided they would explore every option to become biological parents. Dorothy asked me one afternoon, "Why is it that people who don't want children or who shouldn't be parents end up having babies, while some people who want children and who are capable of being effective parents are unable to conceive?"

"It does seem unfair," I said. "I have no easy answers for that one."

Clark and Dorothy struggled with some of the ethical implications of in-vitro fertilization. She was a practicing Christian and he practiced his own brand of spirituality. In-vitro was costly, seven thousand dollars per procedure, and many of the world's people could not afford it. They wondered whether it was morally correct. "If we can't conceive naturally, are we playing God through the use of technology?" they wondered. "What if the doctor can't retrieve one of my eggs? Should we use Clark's sperm and another woman's egg, or her egg and someone else's sperm? That's a choice lesbian couples are currently exercising." Clark's sperm count was low. "Or, should we implant a donor egg fertilized by a donor sperm?" It can become quite complicated with all the options. Dorothy said, "I feel like I'm running down a slippery slope."

When they learned she was still producing plenty of eggs and that they could use Clark's sperm, they decided to proceed. At Dorothy's age, it was lucky to retrieve seven or eight eggs. In her case, they were able to retrieve twenty-five eggs through a somewhat painful process. The eggs were sucked out of the ovaries while she was under a mild anesthetic. Dorothy and Clark were overjoyed and hopeful. Her eggs could be preserved under fertilization for up to a year. One of Dorothy's eggs was fertilized with Clark's sperm. The next step involved trying to carefully insert the fertilized egg through the vagina and implant it in the wall of Dorothy's uterus

They had to wait several days to find out whether the attempt was successful. Dorothy was a bit tender and physically wiped out. Both of them were emotionally drained waiting for the news. I checked back later in the week to learn from a tearful Dorothy that the procedure had not worked. It had been a roller coaster week and she was devastated. Clark was disappointed. My sense was that in some ways the experience bore similarities to a miscarriage. "We have decided to wait a few months and then we will try again," Clark said. The problem is that there are no guarantees. Making a baby isn't always as easy as it seems.

QUESTIONS FOR REFLECTION

- If you or one of your children couldn't conceive and you or they wanted to start a family, what factors would enter into making your decisions on the method? Would your beliefs play a role?

- Do you know anyone struggling with infertility? How can you be supportive?

PRAYER

- Mothering God, having a baby is not what makes us parents but doing the parenting. Help those of us who are parents to love our children with your love and guide us when we want to encourage couples who cannot conceive a child. Amen.

Having an Affair Can Be Attractive and Costly

EARLY IN OUR MARRIAGE my wife said one thing she would not tolerate was "an affair." It was clear from her tone that this breach of trust would be grounds for a swift and sure divorce. In the Lutheran liturgy for marriage, the celebrant quoting Scriptures says, "What God has joined together no person should tear apart." Gail reminded me we both gave our assent to that Word and our promises. Through the years there have been times of temptation for us both, I suspect. I know there have been for me.

Years after this conversation, one of the men Gail worked with at the university began doing nice things for her. Over a period of a couple of months there were flowers in appreciation, later candy because she was so competent, and then lunch because she was a good listener. I began to be nervous and asked her to be careful. She replied, "Martin is just a sweet, thoughtful man." My BS detectors began to quiver. In the following weeks I was even more attentive. One day Gail told me she had learned that Martin and his wife were having problems and he had moved out of the house.

"Aha, I wasn't imagining things," I thought to myself. After she told me about Martin's marriage troubles, I suspect she guessed what I was thinking. Maybe she even recalled our previous conversation. Then she acknowledged the possibility that perhaps her perceptions of the relationship with Martin were not the same as his.

Adultery is the breaking of a marriage vow to our spouse by becoming sexually involved with another person while we are married. I believe the potential for this happening exists in nearly every marriage. Given the right circumstances it can happen. Couples grow apart. They fail to spend quality time with each other. They get caught up in their careers, building a home, raising a family, volunteering in the community. They pursue their own interests and become married singles. They quit talking and listening. Maybe sex ends up being "a quickie" with no romance. They don't pray for each other or with each other. They get bogged down in the maintenance of the house, the yard, the cars, and the dog. They don't care for their bodies and they neglect their minds. They quit growing individually and they become boring.

Late one September I drove with a colleague to a pastors' conference. As we were driving, he said, "Would you like to listen to a tape?"

"Sure. What kind of selection do you have?" I scanned a case he handed me full of tapes. Country western, classical, a few rock groups, jazz, and several by a popular PBS talk show personality. I picked out one on adultery. As the story unfolded, the two main characters were a husband and wife who had been married about fifteen years. The man was a manager of an office, His hair was thinning. He'd developed a slight paunch. He felt stuck in his job. His wife had never lost most of the weight she gained after three babies. She had stopped aerobics and swimming. She had given herself to the kids, meal preparation, and housework and not nourished her inner self. He'd come home from work, read the evening paper, have a beer, eat supper, and fall asleep watching a game on television. She would walk the dog, transplant flowers, and sit and read the *Ladies' Home Journal*. They both had become complacent.

As the story continued, he lost his secretary and an attractive young woman who was hired started working for him. She had just gone through a painful divorce and she shared many details of this loss with him. He was attentive, listened carefully, offered comfort, and felt needed. Slowly an attraction developed between the two of them. They laughed and talked about all sorts of things. Now and then they'd have lunch together or a drink and conversation after work. She felt good when she was with him even though he was just a few years younger than her father. He was planning a business trip out of town and asked her if she'd like to come along. She smiled at the thought of something more than business occurring and agreed to go.

The storyteller continued. When he purchased their airline tickets and made hotel reservations for two separate rooms, he felt a rush as though he were fifteen years younger. "One never knows," he thought. "Something interesting might happen." The next day he began to think about the implications of something happening but they were not what he expected. His children would be devastated and hate his guts. His wife would cry and scream and swear and maybe go to a lawyer. What about the house and his investments and pension fund? His in-laws—well, his father-in-law would probably drive down and break his jaw. Their friends would wonder why he was such a jerk. The gossip would travel through the office, and the school cafeteria, and his Rotary club, and the church. He felt he could never show his face again or receive the Sacrament. His kids were baptized and confirmed there. Slowly he began to realize what he was risking and exactly how costly it would be. Dozens, no, probably hundreds of people would be shocked, saddened, angry, and disappointed in him. Two days later he canceled one plane ticket and room reservation and told his secretary. He was relieved and she was too, sort of.

The great irony of listening to this tape was that my traveling companion told me several weeks later that his wife had been having an affair with a member of his parish council. I just ached for him and their children.

In every marriage there will come times of testing and temptation. Pay attention to your remarks, behavior, and feelings toward another person. If you're attracted, there will be clues or subtle messages sent and received: a look, a note, a flower, a touch. Family and friends can function as an early warning defense line if we are willing to listen to them. I remember once when a congregational leader quietly took me aside and said, "Have you noticed how Wendy looks at you?" I had, because she had written me love notes, but I feigned oblivion.

"How do you mean?" I asked.

He said, "She acts like she's got the hots for you."

"Mmm," I replied. "Thanks. I'll be careful."

I have on more than one occasion terminated a counseling relationship or withdrawn from working in a group with someone to whom I was attracted. I remember telling a female volunteer I was uncomfortable with my feelings for her and she said, "It's not a problem for me. I can handle it."

I responded, "But it's a problem for me and I don't think I can." I refused to work alone with her and she was very angry. It was, I'm convinced, the right thing to do.

I know of marriages that have survived an affair. The road back is long and hard once trust has been broken. Even with the admission of wrongdoing, a promise to end the affair, God's forgiveness, acts of contrition, and a spouse's forgiveness, things are never quite the same. The healing process is delicate and often painfully slow.

It's difficult to remain married to the same person year after year. Crafting a marriage takes time, energy, and care. If you find yourselves ducking issues, drifting apart, and failing to be thoughtful, you can still seek help for your own sake and the sake of the marriage.

In the biblical story, God's covenanting love is always faithful. The people's repeated infidelities are spoken of as adulteries. When we love other people, things, or causes more than God, it's an infidelity. God grieves and seeks to woo us back, but it's always at a cost. Divine love is for me both the model and the resource for reconciling human love gone astray.

QUESTIONS FOR REFLECTION

- If you have ever felt a special attraction toward a person other than your spouse, what were the signals and behavior?
- How could you or did you overcome those desires and feelings and not act on them?

PRAYER

- Holy Spirit, if we are married protect our marriage. Help us in Christ to remain faithful to our spouse because of your faithfulness to us. Where we've failed, wash away our sin and help us to start over by your grace. Amen.

Gay, Lesbian, Bisexual, Transgender, and Queer People in the Church

IN 1993, WHEN I facilitated a series of Sunday forums on the ELCA "Statement on Human Sexuality and the Christian Faith," congregational interest and participation was very high. Most of the anxiety surfaced around sex education for teens, sex outside of marriage, and gay and lesbian relationships. The document was intended to stimulate conversation, which it did. Some people thought the national denomination was selling out to society and ignoring the scriptural teaching. Other people thought we were losing our moral compass and were sending the wrong message to our youth. Still others appreciated the document as a thoughtful attempt to speak for many of the implications of human sexuality. As I looked around the group, unbeknownst to others, I saw a woman whose sister was living in a lesbian relationship after two failed marriages, a couple whose gay son was living in a deeply committed relationship with another man, a family whose cousin and nephew had "come out as gay and been a royal pain," a woman whose brother was gay, a teen whose father was in a relationship with a priest, and a man whose brother-in-law had gone through a sex change and whose wife loved and remained with her former husband. All of these adults were raised as Christians.

The divisions within the church around homosexuality have touched all major denominations. I am not sure why there is more heat around this subject than, say, nuclear weapons, the high profits in the business of selling death in the arms industry, the destruction of our environment, racism, the exploitation of child labor in the sweat shops of developing nations, or the usury and economic exploitation of the World Bank and International Monetary Fund toward developing nations. I suspect it's because our sexuality is so central to who we are as people. If a person's sexual orientation is a given in terms of how they are constituted biologically or chemically, some Christians would argue, "How can we deny people acting out who they are as God's creatures? What harm can be done by two people who love, respect, and serve one another and make a commitment to be life partners, even if they are of the same sex?" This is my belief in 2019. The views of many in the church and society have evolved as our knowledge has grown in the last forty years.

Helmut Thielicke, a Lutheran theologian speaking at a professional leadership conference at Holden Village in the 1980s, said, "Historically the Christian church has had three major responses to homosexual behavior. One is that it's a sin and should not be tolerated in a congregation. Two, that homosexual behavior is a sin but no different than gluttony, greed, prejudice, or lust, and we do not exclude other believers who sin in these ways. Three, that homosexual behavior is not sinful but one kind of response in the range of human sexual behavior. It should be accepted by the church, and homosexuals who seek to live as faithful, committed servants should be welcomed." I grew up with the first two responses, but I've heard the third from more of my colleagues and congregants. Under the Holy Spirit's influence, we have been more inviting and welcoming.

Gays and lesbians have been a source of fear and an object of ridicule, hatred, and violence in both Judaism and Christianity. Their civil rights have been violated in housing, employment, volunteer opportunities, parenting, property ownership, and military service. I believe the church needs to speak out clearly against such injustice. A person's sexual orientation is not a primary factor in their productivity, patriotism, athletic ability, artistic creativity, loyalty, parental effectiveness, or fiscal responsibility.

I know of gay and lesbian Christians whose rights have been violated. That is a justice issue and I would stand with the victims. However, for me the issue for the church is not only one of justice but of morality and faithfulness to one partner. I do not believe, as some do, that the Christian's sexual mores and behavior should be shaped primarily by the Old Testament Holiness Codes around property and purity.

A national church leader who is also a long-time friend said to me, "Gary, what if a Christian couple who were the same sex came to you and asked you to solemnize or bless their union?"

"I would say, 'I am honored that you've asked me.'" A lifelong, loving, serving, forgiving, committed relationship between two gifted people who believe in the Lord and want to serve the church needs the support of family, friends, and the church.

Lydia was discerning whether God was calling her to be a pastor. She was a religion major when she dropped out of graduate school. She virtually disappeared for several years. She had gender replacement surgery. She changed her name to Larry. He spoke with his bishop.

He came out to his home congregation. Larry met with the Candidacy Committee. Then he enrolled in one of our Lutheran seminaries as a transgender candidate.

Larry has completed four years of seminary. He was ordained a Lutheran pastor and called to start and organize an urban mission to the LGBTQ community. He has been making contacts.

Larry has started offering a weekly worship service. He is excited about the interest and the response. I'm encouraged by the synodical support and the affirmation of his ecumenical neighbors. The congregation's name is Spirit Born. I'm grateful for his ministry.

QUESTIONS FOR REFLECTION

- Have you identified some of the gifts of LGBTQ members in your community?

- Do you pray for them in their ministries?

PRAYER

- Jesus, we are all made in the image of God. Guide us by your Spirit that we may discern how to faithfully follow you, live in your love, and be respectful in our differences. Amen.

Sleeping with the Enemy

YEARS AGO, A CHILD I know was fondled by an overnight guest who came into his bedroom. The guest grabbed for the child and groped him under the covers. The child was terrified and feigned sleep and tried to keep pulling away. At the breakfast table the next morning, the mother asked, "Did everyone sleep well?" She noticed a strange look on her oldest child's face.

The guest said, "Oh, Andreas was having a nightmare so I went in to check on him." The guest was a prominent member of his business and church community. When his parents later learned about the incident, Andreas said, "I wasn't having a dream. I was totally freaked out."

His mother said, "How come you didn't say anything to us?"

"Because he was your friend and I figured you wouldn't believe me."

Andreas buried it because of the trauma, until years later a colleague's experience triggered his memory. I was glad his parents had been told.

I stewed over this for several days since I knew the perpetrator and his family. Then I thought that if he did it to one child, he's probably done it to others, maybe even his own children. Three long-distance calls later I tracked down his wife and phoned her. "Sabrina, this is Gary Grafwallner."

"Oh, my goodness, it's so good to hear the sound of your voice."

"How are you doing?"

"Did you know Tony and I are divorced? He lives in the Twin Cities." She proceeded to fill me in on their children, and then said, "What prompts your call?"

"This is very awkward, but I know a family whose oldest child was groped by Tony and I got to thinking about it and wondered if this had happened before?"

It was very silent on the line, and then she said, "Oh, Gary, tell them I'm sorry. It has happened before."

There followed an incredibly painful story. "I knew something was wrong in our relationship. Our daughter came forward at age seventeen and said he had repeatedly fondled her, but he explained it away. I was in denial. Later, a neighbor came over to complain about Tony's behavior with her son and he stopped coaching. Then our oldest son told me, 'Dad did this and said it will help you grow up as a man!' I pressured Tony into counseling and threatened divorce. He went three or four times. I suspected he was abused by his father or grandfather. When I told my folks, they hit the roof. Two of my sisters came forward and said before we were married, Tony had fondled their bottoms. My world was coming apart. Then I received a call from where we used to live and two mothers wanted to bring charges against Tony. Pastor Gary, I wonder how many there were.

"I got a divorce and haven't talked to him for years. He moved away. Our kids love their dad. Our oldest daughter works for her dad, but she won't let him alone with her children. Tony keeps himself very busy and very secluded. He buries himself in his job. I deal with my guilt as a mother. I should have been more perceptive. I have little bouts of guilt." I just listened and ached as she continued. "I've been journaling by the grace of God. My pastor and two friends have been very helpful. It really shakes you up, Gary, to love someone and believe the best about them only to find out it was all a lie. Our youngest son said to his father, 'Dad, if I ever hear you are still doing this, I will haul you into court and prosecute you without mercy.' Our middle son is really messed up. He's a father of two or three children by different women, none of whom he married. He's been in and out of trouble with the law. He hates Tony."

I thought of when they adopted Tim. "Lord, have mercy."

"There are things I wish I could change, Gary. My hair has turned white. I've gained weight."

"I'll bet you still have your beautiful smile."

It was quiet. "Thanks, Gary, you haven't changed."

"I am glad that you are still in the church, Sabrina."

"So am I. It's getting easier."

"I'm sorry, but I just had to call. Thanks for your honesty."

"Can I tell the family we spoke?"

"By all means."

"I'll remember you in my prayers."

"And you too, Gary."

I never would have suspected this esteemed and trusted man was a pedophile. I guess we all need to be more vigilant as parents and grandparents. My heart aches for Sabrina and her children. My heart aches for Tony, the victimizer who was himself a victim. Sabrina has been in counseling and, while the wound is covered over, the inner healing is coming very slowly.

A second story involves a couple with several children. They'd been married fifteen years, childhood sweethearts. He was self-employed. He worked long hours. He traveled a lot. Sometimes he was gone overnight. They grew apart. She was suspicious and asked if he was faithful and he reassured her. She wondered if he was having an affair. She asked him again, and he got defensive but denied it. They talked less and less. He stopped worshipping. She still went to Mass. He left early and came home late. Sometimes he was in the office on weekends.

Then she began to snoop and go through his clothes, dresser, and truck. She found a phone bill with a series of calls from their phone to a long-distance number. She checked them out and discovered they belonged to a woman who worked in a place he frequented. So, she dialed the number, hands shaking, and said, "Hello, is this Lorna?"

"Yes?"

"I am Mrs. Jean Larson. Are you having an affair with my husband?"

After a long silence, Lorna said, "Yes."

There were tears, anger, and rage as Jean slammed down the receiver. She confronted him when he came home and he confessed. She asked him to leave. He refused. The children knew something was wrong. They saw their mother's red eyes and knew she wasn't sleeping well. She wasn't eating regularly. She began to lose weight. She was a nervous wreck. She decided to leave and took the children.

He tracked her down in another state. He pleaded with her to come back. He said it was all over. She had her doubts. He was persistent. He said, "I miss the children." She came back. Things seemed better. Then old behaviors returned and the feeling of distance rolled in like a cold winter fog. She learned that he never broke it off. She kicked him out. She changed the locks. Her girlfriends supported her. She struggled with getting a divorce. Her church said divorce was wrong. He pleaded with her on the phone. He admitted he had a problem. "This woman wasn't the first. It's like I have to prove something. There have been other women over the years."

She pressed him but didn't want to know. "Men, too?"

"A few."

"Women?"

"Dozens."

"And I slept with you," she sobbed. "How could you?"

She went to a clinic and was tested for HIV/AIDS. Her test came back negative.

Her husband told her, "I'm a mess! Don't leave me. I'll go to counseling."

She came to see me on the recommendation of several parishioners. I am not her priest. The torrid tale came out. After an hour and a half of listening, she asked me what I thought.

"I am very doubtful that he can change or that he will change, but he can destroy you." She began to weep. "You still love him, don't you?"

"I do."

She asked me for the name of a counselor and I told her, "Be sure to say I referred you when you call so you can get in."

I didn't see her or hear from her for several weeks. Then I got a card in the mail from the therapist saying the two of them had come in. I couldn't believe the husband was going. His behavior changed. He came around. He asked to visit the children. She said no. She had the tiniest glimmer of hope, but kept her guard up. And one day she discovered a slip with a woman's number. She called her. "This is Mrs. Jean Larson. Is my husband still seeing you?"

Silence. "Yes, he is, sweetie. You feel you're a victim, too."

Jean slammed down the phone. She was screaming when her friend walked in. "He lied. He lied. The cheating bastard. He's sick. He's so sick and I didn't want to believe it. Oh God help me."

The truth be told, he was sick. He is a detached personality, a sociopath, charming, manipulative, a habitual liar and certainly a predator. This is a different chapter, but the same heavy story as the first. She wondered where God was. She wondered how she could ever trust herself or another man after all the years of lies. It will probably take years. Why should she?

QUESTIONS FOR REFLECTION

- Has anything like what happened in either of these stories happened to you or a member of your family, a friend, a classmate, or a coworker?

- If they trusted you with the tragedy, how would you try to respond? Would you ask for help, too?

PRAYER

- Son of God, You healed many of the sick but not all. You also know what it's like to be a victim. Today I ask for your healing love to touch all who have been deceived, used, and abused, and especially for _____. Amen.

Sex after Sixty

IN A PARISH I served, an engineer in his late fifties often worked out at the same time I did at a community center gym. One Saturday morning he asked, "Gary, you know those large pickle jars?"

"Yes," I replied.

"Someone told me the first year you get married you put a bean in the jar every time you make love. In the following years you take out a bean every time you make love." I nodded, waiting for the punchline. "It takes the rest of your life to remove all the beans from the jar." His eyes danced and he had a sheepish grin on his face as he waited for me to reply.

I wish I would have been quick enough to say, "But, Bill, hopefully each subsequent time you make love the quality improves."

His words have resurfaced on the lips of other men over the years. They may reflect some anxiety over impotency. The nature and frequency of sexual intercourse changes throughout the years. Our sex drive or that of our spouse may peak, plateau, or even wane. This appears to be true in all people as well as those who neglect their bodies or don't exercise regularly.

I recall a teacher who married a woman probably a dozen years younger than himself. They played tennis, biked, and were both fairly active. As he began to feel the fatigue of thirty-plus years teaching in a high school and was considering retirement options, his wife's career began to take off. One afternoon while I was visiting in their home he said, "I'm ready to slow down and she's ready to take off in her career." With most of the parenting behind her, she had gone to community college, gotten an AA degree, started working in an office, and eventually completed two more years for a business degree at a private college.

Alice began to move ahead in her chosen field. Initially quite shy, she gained confidence and began to sparkle. She wore snappy outfits, was quite attractive, and began loosening up and laughing. She worked with many men who were her own age or younger. They noticed her and she enjoyed the attention. Her husband became nervous.

One day he came to my office to visit and shared his fear that his wife would fall in love with a younger man. As we visited, he told me that often when they made love, he could not get an erection. If he did, he regularly experienced premature ejaculation. When this occurred, he became more anxious and feared impotency.

I suggested that when they made love Rick not worry about intercourse and reaching a climax but that he hold his wife, stroke her body, and kiss her from her toes to her earlobes. If he wanted to, he could let his penis lie between her thighs, but he should not worry about penetration. He began to relax as the weeks and months passed and he was able to get an erection when he stopped being so anxious. Last I heard he was retired and they were still happily married.

A relative of mine gave her husband a book entitled *All About Sex for Seniors*. You open the book and you're greeted with blank pages. She joked about something that was no longer a part of their relationship. Her husband winced and shrugged, "I don't believe it has to be that way."

Her response was, "Well, that's the way it is, and that's that!" What she meant was, "That's the way it is for me."

One hundred eighty degrees from that perspective was a man whose wife died in surgery after an unexpected illness. They were both in their mid-sixties. He had not planned on dating but he experienced loneliness. Eventually he found himself being attracted to his wife's best friend. She was eight years younger. He told me one day, "You know, we don't live in sin, but if we don't get married something is going to happen."

"Have you proposed?" I asked.

"Yes, that's what we need to talk to you about." There were other reasons they wanted to get married, but it tickled me to know his juices were still flowing.

I didn't know how it would be for my wife and me as we age. Our lovemaking had mellowed and changed through the years. Nevertheless, there was still passion and I hoped it would continue. When it stopped that was a major loss for me. I still miss that part of our relationship. It appears to be one of the losses that can come with aging.

QUESTIONS FOR REFLECTION

- As you and your beloved age, have the two of you talked about new ways to be creative in lovemaking and giving one another pleasure? The setting, different positions, and time of day can all offer variety.

- What would it take to rekindle romance if not making love?

PRAYER

- Oh God, with the passing of time help me not to be boring but a creative and considerate lover and spouse. Amen.

Divorce—It's Not over When It's over

Tom and Terry looked like the ideal couple. They had been married ten years and had four children, two adopted and two biological. They worshipped regularly, sang in the choir, and were involved in various church functions. While they had mentioned periodical struggles around the children, everything else seemed to be going well for the two of them. He was friendly, a good dad, easygoing, and worked as a salesman. She was a planner, a student, athletic, and a loving mother.

When the news of their separation became public, it rippled outward through family and friends like the aftershock of a major earthquake. "No, it can't be," people said. "Not Tom and Terry. We've got to sit down with them and talk. Maybe they just need a time out." Shock, denial, and frustration were expressed by fellow parishioners. Most people were unaware they had tried counseling. Tom knew there were occasional frustrations but every marriage had its pinch points. He was willing to work at it, but Terry had checked out. She could not live with her growing sense of frustration and anger at Tom's laid-back lifestyle. She wanted to get ahead. Little issues, far from being resolved, became magnified. She felt powerless. When I spoke with them, it was apparent her mind was made up.

During the separation, Tom kept hoping that maybe a miracle would occur and that she would return, but she had emotionally moved on. For months he denied it was happening. He kept reassuring the kids that it was just a phase and the two of them would get back together again. Slowly he began to realize that it was over. He grew angry and blamed her and shamed her. A man who had been so easygoing and gracious became critical and sarcastic. All of us who loved them grieved for both them and ourselves.

While pursuing a second degree in graduate school, a professor asked a group of us to go and view Ingmar Bergman's "Scenes from a Marriage." The film traces the story of the lives of several couples and the disintegration of a marriage. Almost imperceptibly you begin to sense subtle changes and a strain in one couple's relationship. Gradually common courtesies are dropped and there is a cooling. Slights occur. Then silences and avoidance surface in their relationship. Eventually the husband says to his wife, "I'm leaving you since I don't love you anymore." Best friends become enemies. As we walked out of the theater in silence, each of us realized that our individual marriages could also dry up and unravel. If you don't think yours can't, you are fooling yourself.

I know there are divorces that occur because of physical or emotional abuse. There are divorces that occur because of infidelity or neglect or an addiction. No one I've spoken with who's gotten a divorce got married with the idea of even considering a divorce. They married forever and there is a sense of loss and often guilt that accompanies a divorce. Both in our Scripture and the teaching of my denomination, I believe God does not want us to live in a marriage that ruins our health because it's exploitive, abusive, or neglectful. Sometimes we marry too young, or we are deceived, or perhaps we choose too hastily.

When a divorce occurs, there is not one divorce but many. There's a physical divorce. Spouses no longer live together or are physically intimate. There's an emotional divorce. There are a wide range of feelings experienced not once or twice but again and again. There is a financial divorce. Income levels and lifestyles can change. There is a familial divorce. Spouses may no longer see their in-laws or even some of their family of origin. There's a social divorce. Friends may treat people differently after a divorce. If children are involved in the marriage, the parenting responsibilities can change. Many of you have probably seen *Mrs. Doubtfire*. I believe Robin Williams played his character so well because he had personally gone through a very painful divorce. It isn't ever over when it seems over.

Most people do not seem to consider a legal separation as an option. Any number have said to me, "It's not fair that I must be single the rest of my life because my ex was abusive, dishonest, a jerk, or unfaithful." In the Gospels, Jesus seems to speak very strongly against divorce, particularly to men who were looking for a loophole. It's as though he's saying in his teaching, "If you choose to marry, it's God's intention that it be for life." Don't enter into marriage lightly. God is the joiner when the two become one flesh. It is both a miracle and a mystery. To break that union not only involves a terrible break but an ongoing cost. You set yourselves up for serial pain. I've seen it in my own family and others.

The one exception for divorce in Matthew and the teaching of Jesus seems to be on the grounds of adultery. Nevertheless, I know many believers or their children who have gotten divorced. The church needs to not let them drift away but to welcome them back by embodying the gracious forgiveness and acceptance all of us have received from God.

QUESTIONS FOR REFLECTION

- Have you observed some people denying problems or being unwilling to ask for help in their marriage?
- If you were or are having trouble in your marriage, do you have two trusted friends you could confide in and ask for their counsel and prayers?
- Can you go to your pastor for outside help?

PRAYER

- O God, be the superglue that holds our love together when the easy course would be to cut our losses and run. Amen.

Choosing to Marry Again

Lawrence and Janet transferred into a congregation I was serving in Tacoma. They had four children. Lawrence was somewhat standoffish. A trucker by profession, he ended up in the construction business as an entrepreneur. Janet served at home, taught Sunday church school, did PTA, Blue Birds, music lessons, and ran a shuttle service. They had sweet children.

Janet was diagnosed with breast cancer in her late thirties. She had surgery and went through chemotherapy. The treatment was tough on her. As a positive and hope-filled woman, she ministered to her nurses, physicians, family, and friends who cared for her. She was a four-year cancer survivor when the cancer returned. She died within a year and a half, a shadow of her former self, pain-ridden with cancer in her bones.

I didn't go back for the funeral since I had accepted a call to serve another congregation in a different state. I did write a letter extending my sympathy and offering my prayers and ear if Lawrence wanted to visit or call. I never heard back.

Eight months after I accepted a call to serve another congregation, he phoned me. I returned his call only to learn he wanted to come up to visit. It was a two-hundred-and-seventy-mile round trip to our house. He drove up for a visit two weekends later and worshipped with us. After the services, we invited him for lunch and we visited and got caught up on his work, family, and spiritual life. Janet's death had been very hard on the children. Even though two were away at college, they all grieved in different ways and on different time tables. Lawrence stayed close to home and in the next few years he was Mr. Mom and still ran his business.

Next he told us he had begun dating. He met a woman at a Seattle Sonics game. Lawrence's friend had given him a ticket he couldn't use. Lawrence and the woman ended up sitting next to each other. They visited off and on during the game and exchanged phone numbers. She was a divorcee with a single son close to the age of Lawrence's youngest two children. She worked in an office and was a practicing Christian. Being conservative, Lawrence moved slowly but he had a plan.

As the weeks and months passed, they began to date and went to movies, dinners, picnics, and sporting events. She wanted to marry and Lawrence was reticent. He said to me, "Gary, I've met so many mixed-up women. They tell you whatever you want to hear. They're so needy. Many of them have been or are still in therapy."

"How about your new friend?"

"She has a self-esteem problem and has been seeing a therapist."

"How do your children feel?"

"The oldest two say, 'Dad, we want you to do whatever is right for you!' The younger two are pretty protective and don't want to lose me."

"Can you take some more time?"

"Yes, I just don't want to make a mistake. I'm not sure what God's will is." I offered to share with him a spiritual discernment process for making major decisions. He agreed to use it. We parted, but I left the door open to further conversation.

Several months later he called and wanted to come up. He told me he was getting closer to marriage but still had some misgivings. He wanted to know if I would come down to "tie the knot." I encouraged him to connect with a local pastor. We were also going to be gone that weekend so it never worked out.

I heard from him six months later. He had gotten married by this time. He volunteered that it was a struggle and wasn't going as well as he'd hoped. "It's going to be more work than I anticipated," he said. I listened, assured him of my prayers and wished him well.

A second marriage is never like the first. A second spouse is never like the first. The chemistry is different. Each marriage takes an adjustment period. You sort through roles, rules, rituals, and expectations. You deal with conflict and learn to negotiate, collaborate, and compromise. Some second marriages grow and thrive. Other second marriages end up being okay with the typical joys and frustrations. But some second marriages turn sour. If children are involved everything becomes more complicated in a blended family. In many second marriages, like the first marriage, there are probably blessings and trials. I'm always happy for those who marry a second time. They have another chance at love, joy, and companionship.

QUESTIONS FOR REFLECTION

- If your current spouse died or you went through a divorce, would you consider marrying again? Why?
- What would you look for in a second partner and what safeguards would you build into the courting process?

PRAYER

- O God, if I/we marry again I want this marriage to be blessed by you and to bless you. Protect me/us from blindness and making a mistake. Amen.

Electing Not to Remarry

THE TWO OF THEM had been married for thirty-some years. All their children were adults who had grown up and moved away, so they were a couple. He came home one evening after working late. A study group of women was meeting in their living room. He was hungry and went to the kitchen to forage in the pantry and refrigerator for something to eat. While he was preparing some food, he heard his wife say to the group, "If Les died I would probably not remarry."

Years before in their marriage, both of them agreed that if either of them died the other would probably remarry if the right person came along. Now his wife had just said she wouldn't. He wondered what had made her change her mind. Was she unhappy with him? Had he failed her? He stewed over her comment for three weeks. One Saturday, he screwed up the courage and asked the question that nagged him. "Several weeks ago, I came home late one evening and your women's group was meeting. I was in the kitchen getting something to eat. I wasn't eavesdropping, but I overheard you say that if I died you would probably not remarry."

"Yes," she replied.

"Can you share with me what's behind your thinking?"

"As a woman, I have never lived alone. I lived with my folks after I finished school and until you and I married. Then I moved in with you. I feel we've had a good marriage. You have been a good husband and father. I don't want to risk marrying a loser and

I don't think I want to take the energy required to build a marriage again."

"So what would you do?"

"I'd continue to work until retirement. I would visit our children and grandchildren. I'd do things with my women friends, travel, and probably volunteer in the community."

That conversation got him thinking, too. He wasn't sure he would remarry either. They had a good marriage. It had weathered the times of testing and dryness. God had been the invisible partner. Marriage was work and hadn't always been easy. Their marriage had matured and gone through various stages. He would miss her support and her companionship. He'd need to learn to do the finances and pay taxes, utilities, insurance, and the Visa card. He would miss her in bed. He would surely miss her practical wisdom, her non-judgmental attitude, her taste in clothes, and above all, her laugh.

There would be certain freedoms, however: Freedom to come and go when he wanted. The freedom to eat when, where, and what he wanted. The freedom from accountability to anyone but God and himself. He'd also be lonely. He'd need a community. Friends would become more important. He might rent a room out to a college student. He might get a dog. He would visit the children, travel, and do volunteer service too. The independence, freedom, and solitude didn't sound too bad. If he became ill, he'd have to tough it out on his own. It certainly sounded less complicated than starting over again. He'd have to be careful not to become self-absorbed. If you've had a good marriage, it's expecting a lot to hit a winner a second time.

I often think of Dennis who worked for the government in intelligence. His first marriage ended in a painful and destructive divorce. He's a teacher and consultant now. He's fun to be with. His two children are grown and he has regular contact with them. He dates women. He's had proposals of marriage. He laughs when I ask him long-distance if he's still single. "I like to go dancing. I like having female friends. I enjoy my social life, but I cannot trust any woman enough to give myself in marriage. I won't let myself be hurt like that again."

"Too bad," I've thought. "You have so much to offer." But once burned, I can respect his wariness to avoid it a second time.

"Gary," he said, "I love God, I love the church, I have my cat. That's enough at this time in my life."

QUESTIONS FOR REFLECTION

- If your current spouse died, would you consider remaining single? Why?
- What might the possible benefits be to remaining single?

PRAYER

- O God, if I have a good marriage, perhaps one might be enough. Amen.

A New Testament Appendix on Our Sexuality and Being God's People

Matthew 19:1–12—Voluntary Celibacy

Mark 10:1–12, Matthew 19:1–8—On Marriage and Divorce

John 4:1–42—The Woman at the Well

John 7:53—8:11—The Woman Taken in Adultery

John 13:1–15—Mutual Service

Romans 12:1–2—The Consecrated Life

Romans 16:16; Thessalonians 5:26—The Holy Kiss

1 Corinthians 5:1–13—A Case of Incest

1 Corinthians 6:12–20—Glorify God with Your Body

1 Corinthians 7:1–16—Directions about Marriage

1 Corinthians 7:25–40—On Virginity, the Unmarried, the Engaged

1 Corinthians 13:1–13—The Way of Love

2 Corinthians 6:14–18—Relations with Unbelievers

Galatians 5:16–26—Living by the Spirit vs. Flesh

Ephesians 5:21–33—The Christian Household

Colossians 3:5–17—Baptism Implications for Relationships

Hebrews 13:4—Honoring Marriage and the Marriage Bed

1 Peter 3:1–12—Wives, Husbands, and a Non-believing Spouse

1 John 4:7–21—The Blessedness of Love

These might be useful for personal meditation or conversation and reflection as a couple or group.

Acknowledgments

SPECIAL THANKS TO CAROLYN Casey for starting the editing process.

My appreciation to Megan Webber for retyping, editing, and helping with the format.

I'm very grateful to Gail H. Grafwallner for her help, support, wisdom, and love.

I'm also grateful for each person in these stories. Their identities have been disguised to preserve their privacy. They have taught me by sharing struggles and victories about living as people of faith who desire to honor God in their bodies and sexuality.

About the Author

GARY GRAFWALLNER IS A Christian pastor in the Ev. Lutheran Church in America. He has served five congregations in the Northwest USA. He has been chairman of the N. W. Synodical Professional Leaders Committee. He teaches prayer, leads retreats, and does spiritual direction. A graduate of the University of Wisconsin, he holds a MDiv from Northwestern Lutheran Seminary, and a DMin from Luther Seminary. He has studied prayer with the Franciscans, the Benedictines, and the Jesuits. He is the author of *Windows*, and *Everyday Epiphanies*.

CPSIA information can be obtained
at www.ICGtesting.com
Printed in the USA
FFHW011158221119
56071548-62079FF

9 781532 697821